# Primary Professional Development

# Circles of Friends

## Colin Newton and Derek Wilson

Folens Publishers

# Acknowledgements

Our joint thanks go to each of our families for all the time out that this book has meant.

Our thanks also go to:
– Gill Taylor who shared in the early development of this work
– Gerv Leyden for his meticulous reading of an earlier draft of this book
– Jackie Dearden who contributed the Circle of Friends story on p.38 – a courageous piece of work.

Many other people have encouraged and supported us in carrying out and writing about Circles of Friends. We won't name them all here – they know who they are. Finally our thanks to all the children and teachers we have worked with, for letting us into their classrooms, trusting the ideas and engaging so honestly in the process. They did the real work.

This book is dedicated to
**Jack Pearpoint and Marsha Forest**

Editor: Karen Westall
Illustrations: Eric Jones

Layout artist: Patricia Hollingsworth
Cover design: Ed Gallagher
Cover image: 'Flemish Fair' by Pieter Brueghel the Younger

© 1999 Folens Limited, on behalf of the authors.

Every effort has been made to contact copyright holders of material used in this book. If any have been overlooked, we will be pleased to make any necessary arrangements.

British Library Cataloguing in Publication Data. A catalogue record for this book is available from the British Library.

First published 1999 by Folens Limited, Dunstable and Dublin.
Folens Limited, Albert House, Apex Business Centre, Boscombe Road, Dunstable, LU5 4RL, England.

ISBN 1 86202 359-X

Printed in Singapore by Craft Print.

# Contents

**Chapter**

**1**

# Introduction and key themes

'In an intact group the pool of shared understandings is like a shared bank account of the group wealth ... Since it is spiritual or psychological wealth, it does not diminish by being spent. Rather, the more lavishly it is circulated, the greater inner wealth and security each single member feels to have.'

Ted Hughes, *Winter Pollen – Occasional Prose* (Faber and Faber, 1994)

## What is this book about?

This book describes an approach to enhancing the inclusion, in a mainstream setting, of any young person ( known as 'the focus child'), who is experiencing difficulties in school because of a disability, a personal crisis or his or her challenging behaviour towards others. The Circles of Friends approach works by mobilising the young person's peers to provide support and engage in problem-solving with the person in difficulty. Circles of Friends is *not* the same as 'circle time' but many of the skills and techniques used by teachers in 'circle time' can be used to support the Circles of Friends process.

**Who is this book for?** Our focus is on the people we are asked to work with, as educational psychologists, the children and young people who are labelled and marginalised in various ways and the people who are paid to teach and provide for them. If you are a special educational needs coordinator, a form tutor, a primary class teacher, a youth worker, a support assistant and you are concerned about the isolation of young people you know with a disability or difference, this is the book for you. It is not about any one label or disability. Ultimately, it is a book for everyone because at some time in our lives, all of us are likely to have needs that are not typical.

**Aims of this book**
- ✔ To provide a highly accessible resource that is both practical and meaningful.

- ✔ For users of this resource to be able to set up Circles of Friends feeling they have sufficient support and guidance.

- ✔ To inspire and encourage interest in creative approaches to the involvement of children in the inclusion of vulnerable and challenging peers.

- ✔ To provide a tool that can reverse pressures to exclude and segregate an individual from his or her school community.

- ✔ To strengthen the processes which help to create and maintain school communities of acceptance to which *all* children truly belong.

**What differences will it make?**

We hope that the successful use of this resource will lead to the following outcomes:

✔ Disabled and challenging pupils will be successfully included in mainstream schools.

✔ Headteachers, teachers, SENCOs, parents and support assistants will feel they have an approach which actually works; increasing friendship opportunities, helping individuals to belong and decreasing behaviour difficulties.

✔ Pupils will feel valued and involved in the support of other pupils that they know are finding school life difficult. They will have become allies in the support of their peers and will feel safer as a result, knowing that they too one day may need such support in their own lives.

✔ Other creative developments in peer counselling, mentoring, mediation and circle time will emerge.

✔ Deeper insight and understanding of disability issues, emotional and behavioural needs and the possibilities of change will develop.

✔ There will be a greater understanding of the need for peer support and teaming by teachers and other professionals.

✔ Reflection and discussion on the themes of inclusion, circles of support for adults, peer involvement and friendship will take place.

**Values base**

This is not just a 'how to' book, although it will give you all the information you need to begin the Circles of Friends process around an individual in your school. It offers an invitation to consider the values that inform your work with young people and to spend time considering why we do what we do and where we are heading with our work in schools. This section makes explicit the values that underlie Circles of Friends work. The values we advocate are those of full inclusion for all; the belief that there is no social justice until each belongs and has an equal place in our schools and communities. But having said this, we must also say: 'We do not yet know how to bring this state of affairs into being.'

This fact is put clearly by Herb Lovett, an American clinical psychologist and writer on inclusive and person-centred planning in *Learning to Listen* (Jessica Kingsley, 1996, p.8):

> '... the idea of a completely inclusive community in which everyone belongs is far more radical than it first appears. In the abstract, many people subscribe to the notion of an inclusive community whose criterion for belonging is that you have to be breathing. In practical fact, however, most of us draw lines somewhere. Notice also that where the line was confidently drawn can in a short time become indefensible and unjust. It is easy to forget that as recently as 1973 pupils with IQs of less than 50 were regarded as ineducable and therefore excluded from the school system in the UK. Inclusive thinking is not easy.'

# Independence and *inter*dependence

Most of us have grown up in a culture which has taught us that competition is a good thing and that independence is a virtue to strive for. We have been taught that those who are unable to 'win' or be independent have something wrong with them and need fixing by experts. This is a 'top down' model of society and has produced a hierarchy in which there are those who know best and those who are deemed to know least. Little wonder that it is hard for us to envision what true collaboration and cooperation might look like. We are also aware of the paradox that is implicit in saying this – after all, this book was written by individuals who, as educational psychologists, are key players in the hierarchy we are describing as part of the problem! It follows from this that we are the ones who are likely to have most to learn.

The quote from Ted Hughes which starts this chapter is a reminder of the difference between 'spiritual or psychological wealth' and monetary or material wealth. The value of material wealth lies in keeping as much of it as you can for yourself, whereas spiritual wealth is enhanced in value only to the extent it is shared with others. Intact groups will include a diversity of voices and there will be some present who do not use language to express their awareness of the world. At the other end of the life cycle many of the oldest members of our families live a separate existence in nursing and retirement homes. Such forms of exclusion limit our ability to generate and circulate spiritual wealth and experience.

## Signing for inclusion

This illustration of the value of diversity in everyday settings was provided by an Infant teacher who is successfully including a pupil with Down's Syndrome in her class. This child communicates by Makaton signing and the class as a whole is learning to use these signs. They are active and enthusiastic in encouraging their classmate to use them also.

The benefits to the disabled pupil are plain. However, there is another pupil in this class who benefits from signs being in everyday use by the group. She is a girl with a profoundly deaf mother and she is bilingual in British Sign Language and in spoken English. Before the arrival of the child with Down's Syndrome, she had felt embarrassed by her untypical signing proficiency and reluctant to admit to having this skill or to share it with others. Since the arrival of another child using signing (the most important thing about the child with Down's Syndrome, in her eyes), she has lost this uneasiness and is happy to share her ability and become a kind of dictionary of sign expertise. In a very real sense, she has experienced 'interdependence'.

# Tales of inclusion

' I can't myself raise the winds that might blow us into a better world. But I can at least put up the sail, so that when the wind comes I can catch it.'

E. F. Schumacher, author of *Small is Beautiful*.

Despite our professed ignorance of exactly what we are heading towards and how we might get there, we are able to bring you some 'tales of inclusion' as signposts on the journey and some glimpses of the bigger picture. We can say something about *inter*dependence and tell stories about how everyone benefits when we try to include. It is important that these stories are told because they are an antidote to so much of what is usually written about difference and disability, and because we know that there are many more such stories waiting to be told.

Unless you are able to subscribe to these values and beliefs at some level, 'Circles of Friends' will be just another name for a bit of imposed social engineering where those in power decide what is best for those who are marginalised.

**Lessons we are learning**

The Circles of Friends process takes a wider look at the relationships in a person's life. As we have looked at this bigger picture, it has become apparent that our usual professional perspective on those relationships has been one dimensional. We have focused on the child or young person solely as someone with special needs who must access the curriculum. But this child is also a son or daughter, a grandchild, possibly someone's brother or sister, a cousin, a next-door neighbour and so on. If we extend this network to include people who potentially share the same interests as the child in question (who love the same pop group, support the same football team, like the same kinds of pets) then we can begin to see that many perspectives on the child are available if only we look widely enough.

# Circles of relationships

Here we take a wider look at relationships. In this model, these are seen as being at four different levels of closeness to the person at the centre of the concentric circles. (This account is based on the work of Jack Pearpoint, Marsha Forest and Judith Snow.)

**Circle One: The Circle of Intimacy.** This is made up of those who are our **ANCHORS** – the people who are closest to us and whom we could not imagine living without. They will typically be members of our immediate family but not invariably so. Younger children may include their pets, especially if they talk and tell secrets to them.

**Circle Two: The Circle of Friendship.** This consists of those who are our **ALLIES** – the people who are friends or close relatives but who did not quite make it into Circle One. These are people we would confide in and would expect to be on our side and stand up for us in a difficult time. They are key to our psychological life support systems and if our Circle Two is sparsely populated, we are prone to feelings of isolation, anger and depression.

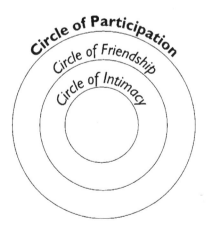

**Circle Three: The Circle of Participation.** This is made up of our **ASSOCIATES** – the people we are involved with because we see them regularly in school classes, at clubs, organisations, in church and so on. These are the people an individual 'hangs around' with; they come and go and may not always be people we see very often.

Circle Three is typically the circle with the largest number of individuals within it. Some individuals who later figure in Circles One and Two will often have been encountered first within Circle Three. 'We met at Dance Class and were married six months later' is a common progression of relationships. Circle Three is the seed bed for close future relationships and, as we will go on to describe in later chapters, it is the members of Circle Three that provide us with the key participants in a Circle of Friends.

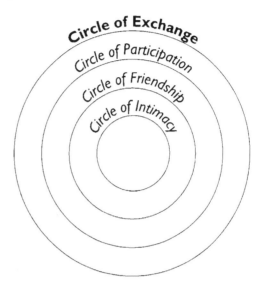

**Circle Four: The Circle of Exchange.** This consists of people who are **PAID** to be in our lives – doctors, teachers, dentists, social workers, therapists, hairdressers, car mechanics and the like. They are paid by us or our caregivers to provide us with services. Children with disabilities and those in care will tend to have higher than usual numbers of people in Circle Four and this skewing of relationships is a serious barrier to their participation in ordinary community activity.

There is a taboo in Western society that discourages the people who make up this circle from moving any closer in relationship to the person at the centre. Sometimes known as maintaining 'professional distance', the result is that the individuals in this circle are unlikely to become close friends or allies of the focus person. The individuals in this circle also have their own agenda as far as the focus person is concerned and it may not always be the agenda he or she would have chosen. Appointment times, caseload management, agency policies, resource availability and promotion prospects set the terms of the relationship with the focus person.

In Chapter 3, we will describe how this picture of relationship circles can be used in the school situation to begin the process of forming a Circle of Friends.

# Circles of support for life

Friends and family: past, present and future ... Some of the most important people in our lives are no longer present with us on a day-to-day basis. They may live a long way away, rarely be seen or indeed may be dead. Present or absent friends and family members continue to play a critical support role in our lives and act as anchors for us as we take risks in our daily lives. They build our self-esteem and are constant internal reference points. These reference points can guide or they can limit, disturb or distort our experiences. Past experience of abuse, loss, separation or rejection may haunt our waking lives and unconscious fears. We may rerun old videos of past relationships in which key people cross in front of our internal eyes and powerful emotions are played out. Still images in sepia, grainy icons of the past, may be current reference points within our circle of living and dead supporters and friends.

Our circles of support change over time. Today they may appear extremely full, while tomorrow we can feel terribly alone and exposed, experiencing loss, isolation, anxieties or depression. This perspective, although focused primarily on children, provides lessons for us all. We all need friends, allies and associates to surround and support us through life. Our families, whilst important, will never be entirely sufficient if we are to reach out and extend our human potential and experience.

**Chapter**

# 2

## Why Circles of Friends?

Circles of Friends is an exciting, fresh approach to meeting challenging individual needs in ordinary mainstream settings such as local schools. The approach promotes the inclusion of individuals who face the greatest risk of rejection or isolation from the community in which they live because of their disability, behaviour or difference.

**Why now?**

Schools, in the last ten years, have faced unprecedented changes and stress and these usually accepting community settings have become, at times, places of rejection and isolation. Innovation overload, significant changes to working traditions, increased autonomy for the individual school and new management approaches have combined with dramatic changes to the way in which schools are financed, measured and held accountable for standards and improvement. One of the unintended consequences of Government legislation in the past decade has been the increasing marginalisation of vulnerable groups. This process has been accelerated by a developing culture of competition between schools. All these factors combine to undermine the confidence and tolerance of many ordinary schools and their staff to make provision for those with awkward needs. (Newton and Tarrant, 1992.)

The need to review methods and approaches that aim to support and include the most vulnerable in our schools has never been greater. The facts of permanent exclusions running at record numbers (official figures from the DfEE for 1995–6 showed a total of 12,500 pupils permanently excluded from English schools – a jump of 13% on the previous year – and in 1996–7, there was a further increase to 13,500) and of increasing pressure to segregate children with challenging behaviour or disabilities are clear for all to see.

Teachers across the world are seeking new ideas to help them solve what appear to be increasingly challenging demands. Governments, too, are calling for advice on ways of increasing inclusion and the recent Green Paper, *Excellence for All Children* (DfEE, 1997) highlights this as a key target for schools to achieve. Yet we lack the practical tools to help teachers support the inclusion of disabled children and to tackle in a meaningful way the challenging behaviour of disturbed and disturbing individuals.

A Circle of Friends provides a powerful way of tackling severe emotional and behavioural difficulties. These difficulties, of increasing concern to educators across the UK, appear to be exacerbated by the within-school factors mentioned above, and major changes within society.

Teachers are therefore keen to adopt approaches which actually bring about change effectively and with relatively minimal adult resource implications.

## Inclusion

*'All means all!'*

There is a growing international movement advocating the basic human entitlement to inclusion in ordinary, everyday community activities including education. There are increasing examples of full inclusion in mainstream education across the world: schools are achieving inclusion of the full range of disabilities and behaviours in ordinary school settings, diverting resources from previously existing special schools and units. Parents of children with disabilities are increasingly demanding mainstream placement for their sons or daughters. Inclusion is the legitimate goal for all children for the following key reasons:

*A human right*

All children share the same basic human right to ordinary mainstream education. Children are no longer segregated by ethnic origin and yet they are by disability. They do not need to be protected from one another, nor should they be devalued or discriminated against because of their disability or behaviour.

*The research evidence*

Pupils with difficulties develop a wider range of competencies in the key areas of cognitive, academic, language and social development when their education takes place in a mainstream setting. More than this, there are benefits for all pupils educated in an inclusive school.

*A meaningful life*

It is essential to take the 'long view' when deciding what is the best education for children and young people labelled disabled. Children with disabilities are more likely to find acceptance and to form meaningful relationships and friendships if educated in ordinary community settings from the start. Continued segregation only teaches mainstream children to be fearful and breeds prejudice out of ignorance.

These points have been summarised concisely and clearly:

> 'Inclusive education is a human right, it is good education and it makes good social sense.' (Centre for Studies on Inclusive Education, 1998)

This vision of inclusion has led to the need for real and meaningful approaches and tools. Circles of Friends have been used in parts of North America and Canada for a number of years to promote the acceptance of pupils with disabilities in mainstream schools.

Within the North American work, the Circles of Friends approach is used as one means of normalising the life experiences of disabled pupils who are recognised as vulnerable to isolation from the ordinary pattern of extended relationships and friendships. This isolation is associated with a system of segregated schooling where pupils' opportunities to know and be known by the wider peer group in their community are limited by their institutional and often geographical separation on the basis of disability.

# What Circles of Friends *is*

Circles of Friends (sometimes known as a 'circle of support') is a **tool for inclusion**. It works by creating the intention to build relationships around the individuals who are vulnerable to exclusion because of their disability, difference or because they face a crisis in their lives. It is a way of building a community that recognises the central importance of relationships and community connections in *all* our lives – for our psychological well-being and for our physical health and resilience. This is the starting point for the work.

No complex psychological theories are necessary. The message is a simple one – relationships are what matter most, whatever labels we have been given, however awkward our needs. There is no cut-off point beyond which someone does not 'qualify' to be included and therefore no one for whom a Circle of Friends could not be built. This is not to say that the community knows how to include everyone – clearly it does not. Too often, acceptance of individual pupils is conditional on their behaviour changing before they are deemed to belong. When attempting to include by building a circle, what changes first is the behaviour of those around the focus person – the person who is at the centre of the circle.

Circles of Friends is not, of course, the only intervention that involves peers to provide support. The 1990s have seen a rapid growth in literature dealing with peer tutoring and mentoring, with peer mediation and conflict resolution schemes, and with peer counselling, particularly as a means of countering bullying in schools. What these approaches have in common is a sharing of responsibility between staff and young people for solving a range of issues that confront every school.

---

## Keep taking the relationships

Research evidence for the importance of a wide circle of relationships in maintaining not just our psychological well-being but also our physical health and resilience continues to accumulate ...

A study monitored 276 healthy men and women between the ages of 18 and 55. They were asked to list up to 12 types of social relationship they were involved in: parent, son, employee, in-law, club member, friend, neighbour and so on. The sample was controlled for factors such as smoking and drinking habits, diets, sleep habits and a range of other variables related to overall health. Each person in the study was then exposed to the common cold virus in laboratory conditions. Sixty-two per cent of those with three or fewer relationships got colds as against only 35% of those with six or more kinds. Why this should be is not known but the evidence is clear – if you want fewer colds, build yourself a wide set of relationships.

**What Circles of Friends *is not***

✔ Circles of Friends is not a new approach to the treatment of any kind of disability or emotional and behavioural difficulty.

✔ It is not yet another attempt to look inside the child and diagnose what is missing or deficient. Viewing people's distress and difficulties and the social context in which they are expressed from the medical perspective alone is seldom likely to be the best way of generating solutions. What we will usually end up with is a list of hypothetical deficits, a clutch of possible labels, a feeling of despair and a lack of a clear way forward.

✔ Circles of Friends is not a behaviourist approach to changing someone. It is at the opposite end of the continuum of interventions from an approach such as 'assertive discipline'.

✔ Circles of Friends is not about seeing the child in isolation from his or her peer group: all teachers are aware of 'vicious circles' of peer interaction that can grow round individuals whose behaviour is challenging to others.

✔ It is not about rewarding or punishing surface behaviours. Circles is about looking deeper, looking behind the behaviour and finding the person. It does not involve looking for deficits in people and attempting to 'fix' them.

✔ Circles of Friends is not therefore something experts arrange for someone else. It is about all our lives. We all know about those times when our own circles of friends have been thinly populated for various reasons and about how this made us feel. All of us have had experience of being 'outsiders' at one time or another, of not belonging or of being excluded and that is a reminder that we all have much more in common than we may realise – whatever our difficulties or differences.

# The role of pupil culture

> ' ... more than any other factor, pupils nominated relations with peers as a cause for both truancy and disruption ...'

> *Talking Back – Pupil Views on Disaffection* (NFER, 1996)

The fact that there is a culture of values and beliefs existing amongst pupils in every school that is separate from what is promoted by staff as the official culture of the school is widely known but little recognised in any of our planning or policy-making. Pupil culture takes some of its identity from the fact that, as a group, pupils are relatively disempowered within their institutions and typically have little say in key decisions. Obviously, pupil culture grows in its complexity and influence as young people progress through the system. In this time, the voice of pupil culture progressively diverges from that of the official culture. As it diverges it becomes increasingly powerful and likely to have a say in whether the 'solutions' to school problems proposed by the official culture are likely to have a chance of success. Consider the following episode.

*A solution from pupils*

A Year 5 pupil, labelled as a child with autism and attending a mainstream primary is regularly involved in fights at playtimes. It is clear to staff that he is finding it difficult to distinguish between 'playfighting' and genuinely aggressive approaches from others and is responding to every advance with real and retaliatory violence. His confusion is also apparent to the Circle of Friends that the school has built around him. On their initiative, they decide that the only way forward is a schoolwide ban on playfighting. They therefore talk to a school assembly about their reasons for the ban and are careful to stress that the focus child is not the only person who finds playfighting hard to handle. Their plea is successful and playfighting steadily decreases during breaktimes. This scenario makes the point that some solutions are only within the gift of the peer group. If the 'ban' on playfighting had been imposed from above and become an addition to the official rules, the chances of it being complied with as readily would have been much reduced.

---

## Pupil culture's interpretation of school 'rules'

This was made plain to Derek during an open evening for parents at the secondary school attended by one of his daughters. A typical city school, it has its code of conduct for pupils displayed on a poster in every classroom. One of its statements is a reminder to pupils that: 'We work as hard as we can at all times.' When Derek asked his daughter if this was really the case, she replied 'No, you do just enough work to make them think you are working as hard as you can.'

---

This is the authentic voice of pupil culture and its importance is that it also has a perspective on the individual focus child. One of the most encouraging things that creating circles illustrates is that the picture of the focus child that emerges, when one asks his or her peers, is invariably richer and more balanced than that typically provided by the adults paid to be in that child's life. All we needed to do was ask.

# Light on additional resources

The key resources needed to create a Circle of Friends are other pupils. If the focus child is a member of a mainstream school, these key resources are already and always there. This may seem like stating the obvious, but the fact is that this resource has been almost wholly overlooked when schools and outside agencies have tried to meet the special needs of individuals. Indeed, the message to other pupils when one of their group is behaving in hard to understand ways is usually: 'Ignore it – it doesn't concern you … ' Whole chapters of Behaviour Management books for teachers are given over to the act of ignoring and teaching the class to do so also. Of course, the other children don't ignore it. They form their own theories about what is troubling the child being ignored and, somewhere along the line, they run the risk of internalising the message that if you are in distress and can't cope, you will be ignored. The Circle of Friends works by travelling in the opposite direction to 'ignoring'. It notices. The other children are invited to give their views and check out their theories. With this starting point, the focus child's peers are often able to come up with successful solutions to a problem situation or an unmet need, if we only ask them and provide support in achieving it.

# Our personal experience

**Origins**

Although no one writer or researcher created Circles of Friends, the approaches described in this book have been strongly influenced by the work of Jack Pearpoint and Marsha Forest of The Centre for Integrated Education and Community in Toronto, Canada. Through their work, we learned of those parts of North America where there are fully inclusive school systems and no separate special provision, and of the tools that had been used to achieve this. We learned of the 'Communitas' group in Connecticut and its sister organisation in the UK – the Bristol-based 'Circles Network'. These two organisations give an international lead in the use of circles of support as a tool to promote the inclusion of people with disabilities.

**Risk taking**

We have found that setting up Circles of Friends in schools has been a rich and exciting venture. We have also found that the work carries its own risks. The approach is relatively new in the UK and we were working with some of the most challenging individual pupils in stressed school settings. The work invites teachers to adopt a particular role. The first risk we faced was trusting the teacher to work effectively with the Circle of Friends that we had initiated. The role of group facilitator ought not to be too unfamiliar, but we have found that some teachers find the gear change from large group teaching to small group work demanding. Others who are very familiar with personal and social development activities have found very little difficulty in running circles effectively.

A more personal and at times very challenging risk has been the exposure of ourselves to work with whole classes of pupils and small circles. Educational psychologists have a background in teaching, but do not have, as part of their role, ongoing experience of class teaching or small group work with pupils. We therefore found facing a large group of children stressful and risky. We risked the situation becoming chaotic, denting our professional reputations within schools as a result, and ultimately letting the focus pupil down.

*Rewards*

In the event, we were rewarded in many unexpected ways. One of the simplest but most powerful was the way in which pupils would run and greet us when entering the school. This is not a typical experience for a visiting educational psychologist whose usual work is discreet, individual pupil-focused and mainly involves discussions with staff and parents.

The risks we had taken to set up Circles of Friends encouraged us to take further risks in our communications about this work to others in the educational world. We took the risk of talking more in the first person and telling our own stories. Doing this allowed us to be ourselves, to be honest as we expected others to be. The following cameo aims to bring alive what this can mean. It summarises an e-mail sent to a national forum for special needs coordinators in mainstream schools, other special educators and psychologists, which was trying to reach out to the people behind the professional roles.

# Beautiful moments

'In the course of work as an educational psychologist increasingly tuning in to the goal of full inclusion, I am beginning to notice beautiful moments in the everyday course of my work ... I wonder if anyone else shares these experiences in such a time of horrendous rejection, segregation and exclusion?

These moments have increased since I have been involved in creating Circles of Friends around vulnerable and challenging individuals and become increasingly aware of the importance of a child's natural community, their peer group and contributions. Take two recent moments ...

✔ Ian, a 15-year-old with no spoken language and cerebral palsy, is adored by his two-year-old sister and plays with his five-month-old baby sister. During a transition plan meeting at a special school ... he beams when she accepts the furry toy he offers ... This is the first time his mum has been in the school for eight years.

✔ Bill, the head teacher, warmly offers a part-time placement for Jenny, a girl of seven with no words but a lot of screaming and severe learning difficulties ... He gives her a school sweatshirt, so that she will know when she puts it on that this is the day for her attendance at the mainstream local school, and talks to her sister about what will happen ... No big fight, no mixed messages ... acceptance and welcome.

Small moments, nothing special perhaps, and yet beautiful in their own way and in potent contrast to so much of the day-to-day grind and battles of work in the special needs world. Has anyone else caught a moment to share?' Replies flowed in and included:

✔ 'If the question was "Am I crazy?" the answer is "It depends". It depends whose criteria we use. By regular measures ... clearly you have lost it ... have given up your personal professional distance. However, according to some of us – congratulations. Now we are all listening. Now we can begin to learn. And incidentally – it's a better way to live.'

✔ Kyra began to speak of her father's terminal cancer. Her mother is alcoholic and Kyra can be a 'little spinning top'. When she mentioned that she finds it hard to go and stay with her dad in case he dies while she is there, Laura moved across the circle, put her arm around Kyra and said 'My Nan died'. Laura held Kyra while she cried.

✔ Matthew refused to draw a Santa on his card. 'I can't do them,' he crossly stated. This went on for 20 minutes with many, many tears. Encouraged, and left on his own, he eventually held up a drawing. 'I like the way you've drawn him fat and jolly', I interjected. Matthew beamed from ear to ear. Kerri started to get cross ... 'I can't draw Santas', and Matthew said 'I'll do it for you. I can'.'

No doubt you will be able to relate to the beautiful moments of your own work with children and also will be aware of the risks you might need to take if you are to begin using Circles of Friends in your own school setting. Only you will be aware of the sensitivities of your particular circumstances along with your own professional and personal skills and experiences. If these include anxieties and vulnerabilities, read on, we are with you.

**Chapter**

# 3

This chapter outlines the practicalities and realities of setting up actual Circles of Friends around vulnerable or challenging individuals. Commitment, understanding and support will be needed from a number of key people, starting with the young person him or herself.

**Taking up the challenge**

The individual embarking upon the setting up of a Circle of Friends around one person is embarking on a challenging and extremely well-intentioned mission. There will be obstacles to overcome and allies to gain, but the benefits and likely outcomes will be worth the investment, however risky it may feel. The scene will need to be set, the key people briefed, the timing and place will be important. All will want to know what the point of all the effort is.

## The main aims

✔ To increase the level of acceptance and inclusion of an individual.

✔ To increase the active attempts of a young person's peer group to intervene positively in that person's life.

✔ To increase opportunities for the individual to make friends in or outside the actual circle itself.

✔ To increase insight and understanding for the individual into his or her own feelings and behaviour.

✔ To provide the individual with a wider range of choices and more sense of control over his or her behaviour in a range of situations.

✔ To provide a *support team* to work actively with and relate to a vulnerable or challenging member of the school community.

## Six essential steps

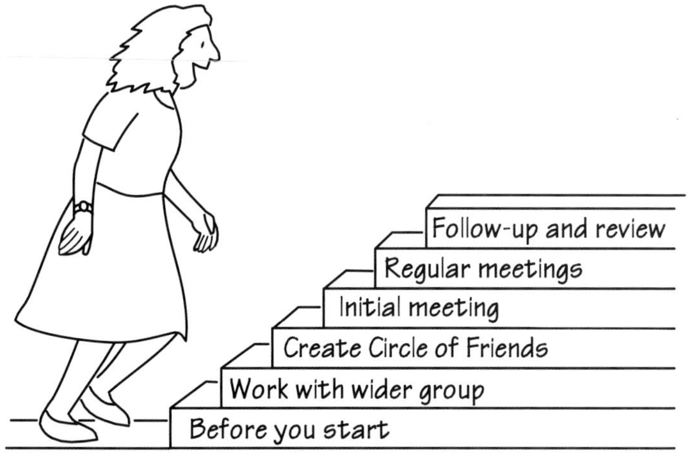

The first three –
1. Before you start
2. Work with the wider peer group
3. Create the Circle of Friends

The second three (*see Chapter 4, p.25*) –
1. The initial circle meeting
2. Hold regular meetings
3. Follow-up and review

These are described in detail in this and the next chapter.

Follow-up and review
Regular meetings
Initial meeting
Create Circle of Friends
Work with wider group
Before you start

# 1. Before you start

**Committed staff**

It is *essential* that the headteacher or senior manager and a key member of staff understand and are committed to using the approach with the young person who is the focus of concern. The key staff member, normally the class teacher or form tutor, must be able to give sufficient time to supporting the Circle of Friends in the weekly meetings that will follow the first meeting of the focus child's class or tutor group. Between 30 and 40 minutes a week will generally be needed. In some situations, this time commitment may be seen as an obstacle, but when contrasted with the time that can be spent on dealing with violent incidents, diffusing temper tantrums and the subsequent exclusion meetings, such time input begins to look minimal. The key teacher may also have to deal with issues that arise from the work for the young person, the group of pupils, for parents or even from other staff.

**Committed parents**

At the very start, before any work is done with the pupil's peer group, the child's parents or carers will need to have had the approach explained to them and to give both their assent and support. New issues may emerge for them, for instance when the phone rings with an invitation or children come knocking on the door requesting that their child come out to play.

**Committed focus child**

The focus pupil will need to have the approach properly explained in a way that he or she can make sense of with a view to the *acceptance* of what is about to occur. We have debated whether the approach could continue with less than acceptance from the individual and we are clear that it should not. When the approach is first described to a child, emotions can range from angry resistance – 'No way ...', through ambivalence – 'well maybe, but what if ...', to over-enthusiastic or unrealistic – 'I'll be cured ...!' Generally, these reactions can be worked through and it is often best to entrust this discussion to a teacher who knows the young person well.

# 2. Work with the wider peer group

There should be an initial meeting with the focus child's class or tutor group.

**The session leader**

In our work, the educational psychologist currently involved with the focus child leads this initial meeting. The meeting typically lasts for about an hour and the class teacher is present throughout and often gets involved in recording the discussion. It is important that someone with whom the class is not very familiar leads this first session. This helps reinforce the message that this is an important session and heightens the interest level. In practice, however, the headteacher, another teacher in the school or even the class teacher him or herself have successfully led these sessions.

**The session aims**

After introductions, the session leader should set out the aims of the meeting. These are to discuss the behaviour of the focus child and think of ways that the class can help him or her. It is worth acknowledging with the class that it is unusual to talk about someone behind his or her back, as is now being done, but that the focus child is aware of what is happening and has agreed to it.

We stress that the session is both unusual and very special. We may be talking about the named pupil this time but it could be someone else in the class on another occasion.

The person leading the meeting can then go on to say that this is a *confidential* session, private to this class. Ask for a definition of 'confidential'. Children usually understand it as meaning 'private', 'keeping what is said inside this room', 'don't blab' and so forth.

It is crucial that the class get the message at this early stage that their help is being asked for, and that the adults genuinely need their insights and ideas. Success depends on this.

**A picture of the focus child**

The leader should now ask the class for their picture of the focus child. Ask for the *positives* first: those things that the child does well and are enjoyed by the class and those times when things usually go well for the focus child. Everything that is said is written up for all to see. We have been continually surprised and encouraged by the ease of eliciting a detailed and positive profile of the focus child. The perceptions of the peer group are invariably more balanced and contain more positive attributions than those from the adult or staff perspective.

Your next step is to ask the class for the things *they* find *difficult* about the focus child, the things they think *he or she* finds difficult or the times when things don't go well for him or her. What is said should also be recorded alongside the earlier list of positives. Sometimes, it can be difficult to get this part of the session going fluently and the leader may need to remind the class that more honesty means a better chance of being able to help. Reluctance may be caused by feelings of loyalty to the focus child or difficulty in believing that adults really want the information that they seem to be asking for. Also, it is probably the first time that they have been asked for their views.

## Who is in your relationship circles?

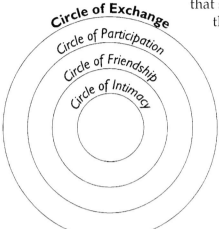

Now that the pupils' perspective on the focus child is complete, the leader of the session moves on to a more general discussion of the role of friendships. The group is encouraged to think about the differing types of relationships that surround them as individuals. We have found it helpful to structure this part of the meeting by using the picture of friendship circles.

They are told that the first circle is made up of those they are closest to and who love them. The second circle is made up of individuals that are close friends, people that they trust and may share secrets with. The third circle is peopled by a further group of friends or acquaintances, individuals that they may meet regularly at clubs, youth groups and so forth, who are part of their lives but not as close as those in the second circle. The fourth circle is made up of people with whom they have regular contacts *and* who are paid to be in their lives such as teachers, dentists, doctors, social workers and therapists.

As each circle is introduced, pupils are invited to think of people in their own lives who figure at each level and these are added to a large version of the figure for all to see.

*Possible methods to use*

✔ Each pupil fills in a friendship circles diagram for their own life using pictures or words.

✔ One pupil is invited to the front of the class and his or her circle is depicted on a large wall chart or on the board.

✔ Pupils are simply encouraged to imagine and think about the circles of people in their lives as they are taken through the diagram as a group.

✔ A volunteer arranges pupils around him or herself in concentric circles to represent dramatically people in his or her life.

So the group is encouraged to reflect on the richness and diversity of relationships in their own lives. The emphasis should be on the quality rather than the quantity of relationships. Care needs to be taken to ensure that individuals with few close friends are not left feeling inadequate.

The next step is a crucial one: to elicit empathic feeling in the group towards those who have very few people in their lives. The group is asked to imagine how they would feel if their second and third circles were empty and that all they had in their lives was immediate family and paid people. This is a powerful part of the session and a rich range of responses is always forthcoming. If prompts are needed, these should focus on the emptiness of Circles 2 and 3, the absence of any friends or anyone to hang around with. Here are some typical responses to the question:

How would you feel?

Lonely ... Bored ... Unhappy
... Embarrassed ... Sad ... Angry ... Like you didn't exist ...
Upset ... Left out ... Invisible ... Unwanted ... As if you had no control
... Fed up with other people ... Depressed ...
Like you're different ... Scared ...

The group leader then asks the class how they would act if they had these feelings. Again, a rich range of responses is readily elicited. If prompting is required, emphasis on the 'feelings' words is all that is necessary. 'How would you act if you felt lonely, left out, angry ...?'

How would you act?

Pupils know how they would behave if they had no friendships. This is the turning point in this whole-class meeting. Older classes (Year 5 (P6) and above) may have made a connection already between what they said earlier in the meeting about the focus child's behaviour and the list they have just generated. This often dramatic overlap in the two lists should be highlighted by the group leader and the class helped to think about whether some of the focus child's difficult behaviour could be a result of his or her feelings about having no friends. This can be an emotional moment for the adults present.

**Ways of helping**

Once the group achieves some measure of insight, the class is asked for ideas on what they could do to help the focus child. Two key tasks usually clearly emerge for the whole group:

✔ Providing the focus pupil with friendship.

✔ Developing ways of keeping the pupil on track with his or her behaviour.

Their suggestions are again listed for all to see. Typically, these suggestions from the class would be included:

> Be friendly ... Welcome him in the morning ... Invite her to play in our games ... Get him into the football team ... Tell her to stop it when she is ... Remember his birthday ... Help him with his work ... Sit next to her ... Don't call her names anymore ... Tell him it's not worth it when he loses his temper ...

This is the beginning of the problem-solving process.

A final optional brainstorming activity is designed to reinforce the openness and honesty stressed throughout. The class is asked to list what is unhelpful for the focus child. (Individuals tend to feel most comfortable with this request if allowed to report what they have seen others do rather than confessing to having done it themselves.) It has become clear to us that this public naming of what can hurt others' feelings is an important and therapeutic part of the process. Often the activities named will involve subtle ways of excluding the focus child.

# 3. Create the Circle of Friends

**Making the selection**  The group leader should now enrol the supporters who will make up a Circle of Friends for the focus child. In our experience, many more children will offer than is needed to make a viable circle (six to eight members is best), so you will need a means of selecting the eventual circle. Several methods can be used to arrive at the final group. Some group leaders like to choose at random from those who have said they are willing to be involved. Others like to make their choices based on the quality of the individual's contribution to the whole-class discussion. Often it is a good idea to take the advice of the class teacher or tutor. Even better, the leader can ask the class itself who they think would be a good choice.

The focus pupil may have ideas about who would or would not be a valuable member, but their views should not dominate selection as others may be in a better place to know who needs to be part of the group. The circle may provide a setting for settling old feuds or for valuing previously disliked others. The focus pupil may be surprised and pleased by who has volunteered or may be initially antagonistic to certain children until trust in the process and clear realisation that all are there to offer support becomes a reality.

Our only advice here would be to avoid choosing only children who are perceived as well behaved by adults. These will likely be children who have had few problems of their own and experience has taught us that some of the most effective and helpful members of a Circle of Friends will be those who are seen as being quite 'difficult' themselves.

## Variations on a theme

The particular process discussed above is the one we have found most effective for a focus child who is showing challenging or isolated behaviour. With a few minor alterations to what is said by the group leader, the whole-class session can also be run to enlist support for a focus child who is about to start as a new member of the class – often because he or she has been the subject of a permanent exclusion from another school. The key questions for the group would then be: 'How does it feel when you are the new person in a situation where everyone else knows each other?', 'How might you act if you felt like this?', 'What are the things that people can do that are helpful to someone who is new?' and so on.

Likewise, the session could focus on the needs of a child within the class who is experiencing learning difficulties with a view to establishing a circle of learning support. Key questions here could begin with: 'How does it feel when you don't understand what to do?' and then follow the typical sequence.

**Help from all**

With the Circle of Friends now chosen it is worth reminding the class as a whole that, although they might not be in the circle itself, they can still be helpful by being friendly towards the focus child, supporting the circle members and by trying to carry out the strategies they have already suggested in the brainstorming session. They also may have created a reserve list for the circle itself.

The whole process may only have taken an hour but the effects can be far-reaching. This whole-class session is central to the process and acts to sensitise the group to the needs of the focus child. Things are now out in the open and can begin to move forward. It will now be much harder for individuals to join in with teasing, excluding or victimising the focus child even if they are not part of the Circle of Friends proper.

Arrangements now need to be made for the first meeting of the circle together with the focus child. This should take place as soon after the whole-class meeting as possible.

**Chapter**

**4**

The circle in action

There are many ways of running small groups with a focus pupil at the centre. The approach we describe is only one way into this. Readers may develop their own process. Be creative but adhere to the key principles:

- ✔ The circle is present to support the individual's inclusion.
- ✔ Respect the dignity and human rights of the individual focus pupil however challenging his or her behaviour.
- ✔ Ensure that there is mutual support and trust.
- ✔ Encourage openness and honesty about feelings and behaviour.
- ✔ The focus pupil must feel listened to and supported, not simply challenged or threatened by the process.

## 1. The initial circle meeting

The initial session with the circle of volunteers sets the scene and is thus very important for all involved. The first session should be carried out as soon as is practicable after the whole-group session outlined in the last chapter. Delay will only raise concern or anxiety in the mind of the focus pupil or undue over-excitement in the potential Circle of Friends.

The first session must feel safe for the focus pupil who will experience the full *spotlight* of the peers' attention while talking frankly not only about what they like about him or her but also regarding behaviours they are unable to tolerate.

### Suggested approach to running initial session

- ✔ Introduce self.
- ✔ Agree ground rules and explain confidentiality.
- ✔ Agree aims of group, e.g. to help focus child make and keep friends and to help him or her get back on track with his or her behaviour.
- ✔ Invite group members to tell child why they volunteered to be in the group.
- ✔ Elicit and list positives and areas the child needs to work on from the group.
- ✔ Brainstorm strategies.
- ✔ Agree which strategies can be tried and ensure commitment to these from the group. Be clear with the group about responsibilities, disclosures and boundaries. Let them know what is expected of them and the limits to this.
- ✔ Agree name for the group, avoiding child's name. The Tigers Group, The Helpful Group, The Listening Group and The Eclipse Group are some examples of actual choices.
- ✔ Describe meeting and follow-up arrangements and encourage mutual support in the group.

**Introductions**

The focus pupil should be well prepared for this initial circle meeting. This is best done individually before the whole-group session is run. An adult, such as the class teacher or tutor, is usually best placed to carry out this pre-session counselling. The key principle to bear in mind is that the focus pupil should not be shocked or surprised by what is being discussed with him or her. The session begins with introductions and sometimes with a warm-up activity.

**Ground rules**

Ground rules are introduced next. As in the whole-group session, confidentiality is both discussed and defined. It is explained that any one of the circle members could be sitting in the focus pupil's chair at some point in the future. What is being discussed is thus highly confidential to the group unless essential to the interests of the focus pupil.

Other ground rules are introduced at this stage. All rules need to be kept simple and meaningful, and might include these:

✔ Only one person speaks at a time.

✔ Act sensibly during session.

✔ Keep confidential what is spoken about during the session unless something is shared which is so important that it has to involve others.

**Aim**

The aims of the circle should now be clarified and restated for all present, including the focus pupil. Again the aims need to be simple and straightforward. Typically, aims might include 'getting Ruth back on track with her behaviour' and 'we are going to try to help Ruth make and keep some more friends'.

**The volunteers**

The next stage is often one of the most moving of the whole circle process and certainly of the initial circle meeting. Each individual circle member is asked to explain in simple terms why he or she chose to volunteer to be a member of the focus pupil's circle.

---

## A risky start

Colin was very anxious as he sat down with his second Circle of Friends ever! He awaited in some trepidation the arrival of the focus child who was being brought to the room by his class teacher. The circle was getting restless, when outside the door could be heard a tremendous commotion. Colin felt a sinking feeling in his stomach, which was compounded when the door was thrown open and the focus pupil, Richard, was thrust inside by a red-faced teacher spluttering the words: *'He's all yours now, I'll be back at 12 o' clock!'*

Colin agonised as to whether he should call a halt immediately. He decided to continue. Richard curled up in his seat in the circle looking extremely angry and resentful. He was finding it hard even to look up or give anyone eye contact.

Having decided to proceed, the early question was posed as to why pupils had chosen to be part of his circle. By the time the fourth child had explained why he chose to volunteer to be a member of Richard's circle, he had opened up like a small but very precious flower!

**The positives ...**

One effective way of beginning to create an honest dialogue between the focus pupil and his or her peers is to revisit the questions posed to the whole group within this initial circle meeting. The question: 'What do we like and value about this person, what are the positives?' will usually invoke a very constructive brainstorming activity. Someone needs to write down or use graphic images on a large sheet of paper for all to see the responses to this question. The adult facilitator can make much of positive comments, can extend specific praise or even add his or her own observations.

**... and the negatives**

The circle needs now to examine situations where things have not gone well for the focus pupil. We have tried to avoid this becoming a long list of negatives and labels attached to the pupil concerned. Focusing on situations, rather than deficits or personality traits, seems more useful and less damaging for the individual. However, there should be no avoidance of straight, honest talk. It is crucial during this discussion to ensure that the individual continues to feel safe and not excessively threatened by this feedback as this could cause resistance. Methods of maintaining a safe climate in this situation include the following:

✔ Keep the list of difficult situations quite short.

✔ Explain in very clear terms to the focus pupil that what may be said is only what an individual feels or has experienced, it is not necessarily true, and the child should not be surprised if he or she does not agree. The circle will not be spending lots of time trying to work out what was or was not done by an individual in any given situation!

✔ Use humour to lighten up potentially difficult contributions.

✔ Challenge quickly any rule-breaking or direct attacks between members of the circle.

During this process, beware of possible sabotage from circle members bringing their own agendas into the meeting. Watch also for problematic relationships overflowing into the circle meeting itself. Old feuds, hurt feelings, resentful victims and individuals looking for revenge, all bring their own risks and tensions to the meeting. This format gives plenty of opportunities if individuals wish consciously or unconsciously to make the situation difficult for the focus pupil, and so the onus is on the facilitator to keep the meeting safe for all present.

**The strategies**

The next stage is to brainstorm strategies to support the focus pupil. Ideally, the focus pupil him or herself should be actively involved in contributing to this process, but it is only natural that in the initial meeting many individuals prefer to be largely silent. As above, the adult(s) present should record all ideas in words or in graphic images and, after a period of brainstorming, return to the ideas and refine them with the group. These are the key principles that underpin this process of strategy creation and acceptance:

✔ Ensure that individuals own the strategy they are suggesting. As far as possible, avoid other people being named who need to carry out the strategy, such as the class teacher.

✔ Ideas may need nurturing and developing by other group members or the adult running the group.

✔ The consequences of some ideas may need to be explored, especially if they could be counterproductive.

✔ Ensure that the focus pupil is able to accept the strategy and that he or she will cooperate with it, at least in principle, during the meeting.

✔ Commitment from circle members to strategies and ideas is essential if they are to be carried out in the real world.

**A name for the group**

Before closing the initial meeting, it is important to agree a name for the group. The circle should not be referred to as the *Circle of Friends* or in a way that includes the child's name. A more neutral title is preferable. Examples that have been used include the *Listening Group*, the *Reds*, the *Support Team*, the *A Team*. Circle members can generate ideas but ideally the focus pupil selects the circle name. The circle name is important for the group's identity and reinforces the mutually supporting aspects of this work.

**Future arrangements**

Finally, at the close of the initial meeting, follow-up arrangements need to be agreed. A meeting place, timings and availability of the adult facilitator and circle members need to be established. This meeting has been the first of a series of weekly meetings and this should be clearly stated.

Immediately after the circle breaks up, it is important to speak briefly to the focus pupil to assess the impact of this first session. If it has raised issues with the young person, a longer discussion may be required. Quite possibly, circle members will want to leave the room with the focus pupil and clearly we do not want to disrupt this unnecessarily.

# 2. Hold regular meetings

A weekly meeting with a key member of staff has now been set up with the six to eight volunteers. The initial meeting is usually facilitated by the group leader who has carried out the whole-group session described above, together with the teacher who is to run the group, observing and helping to record responses. The first meeting usually requires 45 minutes. Future meetings can run for approximately 20–40 minutes. Some circles have been successfully run during playtimes, assembly times or even, at a push, during registration in at least one secondary school.

A range of approaches can be used for subsequent meetings. Problem-solving processes work well and are usually relatively safe and easy to learn for all involved, and these should also allow space to explore difficult issues and celebrate successes. A main purpose of the meeting is to generate supportive ideas and practical tactics. The initial group facilitator – a visiting educational psychologist, support teacher or other – who has introduced the circle to the whole class needs to meet the class and the circle itself by the following half term or term end to follow up progress.

**Possible problems**
Early meetings of a Circle of Friends can be chaotic and difficult for the adult to manage constructively. Angry feelings towards the focus child are sometimes expressed or discussions are begun that have no obvious relevance to helping the child. The adult needs to remind the group of the ground rules, the reason why they are meeting and of the need to listen to each person's contribution.

For younger children (Year 3 (P4) and below), it can be helpful to structure the group meeting in ways that make the listening and turn-taking roles clearer, for instance by having warm-up and closing routines, by asking for the group's comments on set questions or by allowing group members to talk only when in possession of a special object. Objects may include a talking stick, a listening stone, a pretend microphone and so forth.

We encourage people running Circles of Friends to follow their instincts, drawing on their own gifts and experiences of talking with and working with children. Adults should have a genuine commitment to the focus pupil and be able to listen to and follow the lead of children. The focus pupil should be very carefully listened to and as far as possible increasingly allowed to guide proceedings to ensure that their needs and issues are addressed.

**The need for clarity**

We have found that there is a need for clear boundaries regarding how group members deal with disclosures from the focus child. The adults may wish to give clear permission for circle members to pass on any information disclosed to them that they feel they cannot keep to themselves. This may be particularly relevant to children with a history of abuse or who are believed to be at risk.

Permission and guidance is helpful with regard to what the circle members should put up with from the focus pupil. It is important to stress that they continue to have personal rights, which should not be violated. It is not acceptable for circle members to be abused physically or verbally just because they are trying to support and they need to hear this early on.

Group processes and content can vary enormously and are largely influenced by the style and strengths of the facilitator and what he or she feels able to handle or pursue. These can range from deeply emotive material to 'straightforward' behavioural strategies.

# 3. Follow-up and review

There is an important need for maintenance, support and follow-up sessions and for any involved outside facilitator to keep in touch, especially with a newly formed circle. Structured support, and even supervision where necessary, may be provided by some outside facilitators to those carrying out the weekly facilitation. It is well worth teachers negotiating for this, especially if new to this type of approach.

**The circle facilitator**

The circle leader or facilitator should contain, hold boundaries and ensure safe space for the exploration of feelings and ideas. The role is also to provide rich positives and praise and to build the esteem of the individual and the circle. The facilitator should attempt to encourage mutual support, trust, honesty and openness among the group members. This role is crucial to the success of Circles of Friends.

The commitment, skills, personal qualities and model provided by this adult deeply influence the progress of the circle in its acceptance and support of the focus pupil. In order to carry out this crucial and at times complex role, the facilitator ideally needs support and supervision in his or her work with the group from someone with appropriate psychological skills and strengths. In the busy 'real world', this may not be possible, but identifying a trusted colleague to confide in and be supported by, plus close contact with the outside facilitator if a visitor, or another member of staff with experience of group work, is essential. We all need people for support in much the same way as the focus pupil. Jack Pearpoint and Marsha Forest favour the rule of the scuba diver: *Never dive alone!*

*The need for supporters*

This is excellent advice for the teacher running the Circle of Friends sessions. It happens to be excellent advice to pupils within the circle also. Jack and Marsha developed this rule whilst scuba diving in Mexico. Colin learned from a British diver that diving in UK waters is particularly treacherous.

The sea is often extremely murky. In such circumstances, divers not only always dive in pairs but regularly tie their wrists together by a length of rope. Added dangers in British waters include sunken wreckage, old fishing nets and various other debris! The lesson is clear: be especially careful not to dive alone in risky situations in UK waters! (After all, who has been able to see their hands in front of their face in the murky waters of British education over the last ten years?)

Working together, circle members are also more likely to be more effective with the focus pupil. Pairs are much less vulnerable to intimidation, bullying or aggression from a highly challenging focus pupil who is being supported.

## Never dive alone

One pupil, Brian, complained of being hurt quite badly when he had been alone with Scott whom he had invited to his house. He had, however, really enjoyed playing with him and had visited Scott at his home. The solution was not to stop inviting Scott but rather to include Paul, who was another circle member, in the visits.

**Pupil interventions**

We have been greatly impressed by the richness of the discussion and the way the group has functioned in circles, often surpassing adult problem-solving and mutual support-giving. We are also struck by the power of very simple interventions from other children. For instance:

*I just say forget it ... and she does.*

*We just follow him out of the room and quietly ask him to come back ...*

*I went round to her house and asked if I could play ...*

*I saw him in the supermarket and I specially tried to talk to him ...*

Other interventions range from the rich and varied to the mundane and adult-oriented. We are fascinated by interventions occurring outside the classroom:

*We saw him getting angry with the dinner lady ... we went and started talking to him .... told him it was not worth it ... he walked away.*

*I told him to go back in and apologise to the teacher ...*

and even outside the school:

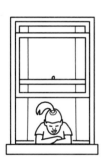

*I leant out of the window and shouted 'do you want to come swimming, Shane?' He said he couldn't, but now he comes every week with us.*

Many of the pupil-generated strategies are creatively preventative:

*We've invented a 'three tap code'... if he starts talking on the carpet, one of us taps the floor near him ... then he shuts up.*

*We are going to design a chart and write how well she has done during each lesson.*

*Wayne is going to sit on one side of him and I'm going to sit on the other ...*

*We are going to speak to Samantha because she is making her life really bad ...*

Active interventions with the adult world reveal new insights into pupil perspectives on supply teachers, class teachers and midday supervisors, but are also excellent ways of calming difficult situations:

*We need to invite Mr Rogers [head of year] to our next meeting to talk to him about how he is treating John.*

*We are going to write a letter to her mum ...*

# Developing circle meetings

There are a range of additional ideas and resources for those wishing to expand their repertoire of processes beyond what they can instinctively carry out or plan. Nevertheless, Circles of Friends is unlike any other group that has been set up before, so a willingness to explore and be creative, whilst respecting the pupils involved, will continue to be the most essential. One approach which lends itself well to this work is the *problem-solving approach*.

Most group problem-solving approaches follow variations on the following sequence:

✔ Review positives and negatives.

✔ Agree problem area to work on.

✔ Select and specify target.

✔ Brainstorm strategies that will help the achievement of this target.

✔ Select useful and workable strategies.

✔ Agree who will do what and when.

✔ Ensure focus pupil is comfortable, involved and accepting of agreed targets and strategies.

Another source of ideas can be drawn from Personal Development approaches.

Specific strategies for strengthening the circle and facilitating its problem-solving can be found in Bliss and Tetley, *Circle Time* (Lucky Duck Publishing, 1993), Mosley (1996) and White, Developing self-esteem in Bovair and McLaughlin (eds), *Counselling in Schools – A Reader* (David Fulton Publishers, 1993). These authors describe activities for use with children which promote the Personal Development curriculum via the use of group exercises known as 'circle time'. Amongst the key areas explored are relationships with others, issues of individual identity and responses to challenging experiences.

Useful techniques and processes may be drawn from some recent work that has focused on Social Skills developments in small groups.

Psycho- and socio-dramatic group processes lend themselves to work with Circles of Friends perhaps in relation to particular social situations that need acting out and reframing.

Therapeutic approaches towards group work derived from the humanistic, psychodynamic and counselling traditions may also be highly relevant at times. Gerda Hanko's (Hanko, 1995) work with teacher problem-solving groups is particularly relevant given the stress she places on the role of the group facilitator and the need to encourage the group to ask 'answerable questions'. Whilst these are not therapeutic groups, some of the circles seem to offer individual children opportunities to share their deepest secrets, sufferings or vulnerabilities in a healing way.

# An aide-memoire for effective circle facilitation

✔ Take care that the circle does not get into the habit of racing from issue to issue as it discusses the previous week. Effective problem-solving depends on allowing time for a deeper exploration of the key areas of tension and difficulty.

✔ Learn to live with ambiguity and uncertainty over outcomes. Remember that, as the adult present, you are only likely to know the outlines of the issues, not the detail. Premature solutions, reached without a full exploration of the issues, are likely to be ineffective. Stick with 'not knowing what to do' for a bit longer.

✔ Be watchful that the focus child is not overwhelmed with questions and suggestions from the circle. The focus child is not 'on trial' and it is seldom helpful to be asked to 'explain yourself'.

✔ Leave space at the end of the session to ask if there are any worries that have not been talked through. If the 'real worries' tend to get an airing only at the very end of the session, you need to spend more time building trust within the group and encouraging them to listen supportively to each other.

✔ Remember that the circle is unlikely to arrive at a solution for everything that may be a concern. Encouraging circle members to ponder over questions between sessions can often be a helpful way of moving things on.

✔ Keep the focus on what is being achieved and how. Say what positives you have noticed and those that other staff have reported to you.

✔ And the *Golden Rule* – resist the temptation to give the circle your 'good advice'. Your role is to support them in arriving at *their* best solutions, not yours.

**Graphic facilitation**
There is growing interest in a method of facilitation that involves the use of a large coloured graphic to record the problem-solving process. A large sheet of paper is taped to the wall and serves as a focus for the group's discussions. The person providing the graphic facilitation makes a colourful record, using words and pictograms.

This can be a very useful aid to the running of the circle meetings and offers the following potential advantages:

✔ The richness and complexity of the whole can be seen at a glance.

✔ Links can be visually identified and connected.

✔ It is applicable to people who do not use language in typical ways.

✔ The final display becomes a group memory and can be built upon subsequently.

✔ Individual contributions are respected and valued by the act of recording. This enhances individual involvement.

✔ Latecomers to the meeting can 'catch up' quickly and those who need to leave early can revisit the discussion that they missed.

✔ Visual stimulus activates other modes of thinking.

✔ The graphic display can confirm the accuracy of what has been recorded and alter it if necessary.

✔ At a subsequent meeting, the group can quickly pick up where it left off.

✔ Colour is used to reflect and emphasise feelings.

# Chapter 5

## Outcomes, stories and a theory

In this chapter, we share some of our experiences of Circles of Friends in action. We explore some of the outcomes for focus pupils, other circle members, staff and ourselves. The outcomes described are diverse. This emphasises the need for staff to be open-minded about the ways the circle's work will evolve. As one headteacher said to us about his experience of running Circles of Friends, 'Things can get a bit wacky at times'.

## Some case studies

**Christopher's story**

Christopher was a Year 6 (P7) boy attending an inner-city primary school. He had had behaviour problems since attending nursery. The same themes were present in Year 6. Christopher continued to present temper tantrums, lack of self-esteem, zero cooperation and extreme aggression, and was someone who found losing games very difficult to handle.

Staff and services involved with Christopher and his family had suspicions of physical and emotional abuse, but these were never substantiated despite numerous explorations and constant close monitoring. Christopher's parents were extremely difficult to work with. His dad was very aggressive and it was hard to get him to sit down, let alone to listen or enter into dialogue. Christopher's mum seemed anxiously protective of her son and also found it difficult to listen for that reason.

Colin had been the educational psychologist for four years and had become extremely frustrated with interventions aimed at changing Christopher's behaviour. Work with parents, behaviour programmes, target setting, reward systems and a number of other interventions had been unsuccessful. The pressure to exclude Christopher permanently grew every year. A number of teachers had found his behaviour very stressful; one had been very close to a nervous breakdown and he put this down to Christopher's presence in his class. He reported waking up in the night and picturing Christopher in front of him.

All in all, this was not a very encouraging place to start. Yet after four months of work in a Circle of Friends, Christopher had changed!

At the start of the first circle meeting, Christopher had been extremely tense and his body was wound up on his chair. However, by the time the fourth pupil had explained why he had volunteered to be part of his circle, Christopher had relaxed.

*Progress is made*

Within a few weeks, Christopher was no longer presenting serious tantrums. He was much better at participating in sports, more able to take the stress. He no longer talked out of turn in class. When unhappy about something, he was quicker to tell someone. Christopher had also found a new 'best mate' from a class member outside the circle.

A year later, Christopher volunteered for membership in a Circle of Friends for a pupil at his local comprehensive school. He was happy to say that he had been part of a circle in the past for himself and that this had helped him to stop hitting people and to keep him out of trouble. Two years later, Christopher continues to be successfully included in his local comprehensive school despite facing a range of challenges there. He recently recognised Colin in the school's Support Centre, saying: 'You're that man who does friends of circle, aren't you?!'

## A Circle of Friends in a first grade classroom

In 'A Circle of Friends in a first grade classroom', *Educational Leadership*, 48 (3), (1990), Susan Sherwood provides an example from North America of creating a Circle of Friends for a six-year-old with severe multiple disabilities following birth trauma and head injury. Ann had moderate to severe learning difficulties, no right field vision and only a small amount of left peripheral and central vision plus a right-sided hemiplegia.

*Peer support*

Susan was amazed at the ability of first grade pupils to provide a structure for Ann and appropriate activities despite the absence of an adult support assistant. For example, when another pupil, Mike, noticed that Ann needed assistance, he would gather the necessary materials, quietly approach her and firmly direct the task. On one occasion when she flatly refused to participate, he unemotionally prodded her,

> 'You have to because you're a first grader, and these are the things first graders do.'

Then, without a pause, and with the same sense of purpose as an adult, he directed her to trace the letters.

Susan concludes her description of the approach with the following thoughts:

> 'As I reflect on this past year, I know that Ann's life has been touched in many ways by her peers and teachers because she was afforded a free and public education in a regular classroom. Yet the integration process isn't easy. At times, it can become all consuming. With no right answers, however, we cannot allow ourselves to be constrained by past practice. Don't be afraid to try. My vision for education is students, parents, educators, and administrators working positively to make learning positive and empowering for each student within a regular classroom.'

## Simon's first circle

Simon was a Year 5 (P6) pupil in an inner-city primary school. He had been given the label of Asperger's Syndrome. Simon was experiencing great difficulties in being able to trust and respond to his peers in the ways in which they would expect him to.

Consequently, he was being 'wound up' and 'excluded' by his peers. There was considerable concern that Simon was not coping in his school. However, he was clearly stating that he wanted to stay and he was distraught when his parents decided to keep him off school. After a great deal of negotiation between Simon's parents and school staff it was agreed that Simon should have a Circle of Friends. Simon's mother and particularly his father were not sure that a Circle of Friends would be beneficial to Simon and were insistent that neither they nor Simon would want his disabilities highlighted. In their view, all Simon wanted was to be accepted as he was.

Jackie, the educational psychologist involved, arranged to initiate the Circle of Friends with Simon's class group and to facilitate the first small group meeting. During the whole-group session, Simon arrived in school with his parents and they insisted on speaking with the educational psychologist before the small group meeting took place. Jackie went to meet them amidst an air of anxiety and tension from both school staff and Simon's parents. The pupils who were to form the circle were waiting to talk with Simon in one room, together with the special needs coordinator and the special needs support assistant who were to be involved in supporting the Circle of Friends. In another room, Simon and his parents were talking with Jackie. Simon's father was angry; his son had been bullied and in his view nothing had been done. He explained that his son did not trust people easily and did not think that he was going to trust a group of six pupils. Simon's father did not want Simon to meet with the small circle.

*Parental involvement*

Jackie suggested that if Simon would find it difficult to meet the small group on his own, perhaps his parents could support him by being with him. Simon's parents agreed to take a big step and accompany their son into the next room to meet the support circle and staff.

Simon's peers were open and honest. Simon's parents listened. Emotions were laid bare. The young people in the room felt responsible. Simon's father felt angry but he believed the young people really did want to help his son. There was an intense feeling of caring from everyone in the room. Helping ideas flowed and Simon was clear about which ones he liked and would *accept* from the group. Simon's father spoke from the heart; he thanked the young people and shook each of their hands in turn.

Simon's circle continues to make a difference. Without the inclusion of his parents, it would not have been able to exist.

# A long time coming

When the effects of what we do are far removed in time from our original actions, we typically have difficulty in seeing a connection. We are becoming increasingly aware of this failure to make links when the cause and effect have to do with our treatment of the environment, but we still need reminders that the effects of our *social* actions also may not be apparent until many years later. Consider the following research finding:

David Quinton, in 'The consequences of care: Adult outcomes from institutional rearing,' *Maladjustment and Therapeutic Education*, 5 (2), (1987), studied the adult adjustment of young women who had grown up in institutional care. He looked for factors that would help distinguish between those women who had achieved a relatively settled adult life, partly because they were able to make *planned* choices, and those whose lives were chaotic, marred by unstable and unsupportive relationships and who made few plans. A key factor that distinguished the groups was that many more of the women who had achieved some stability in their adult lives reported having had *positive experiences in school.*

Somewhere along the way the women who had done best had a teacher who had believed in them and managed to give them a sense of personal achievement. An encouraging finding, but Quinton's data enabled him to draw a further and much less obvious conclusion. He had teacher ratings of the girls' behaviour and adjustment during their school years. There was no evidence from those contemporary ratings that teachers' actions and efforts on behalf of the girls was having any effect on their behaviour *at that time.* Quinton concluded: 'People caring for such youngsters need to know that their efforts may well increase the chance of a good adult adjustment even if they do not seem to be having much immediate impact.'

## Kim's circle: A headteacher's commitment was crucial

Kim, a Year 4 (P5) pupil, and her family had moved to the city to escape continual physical abuse and violence from Kim's dad towards her and her mum and brothers. Her current school and home address were her third within a year. At each new address, there had been major difficulties with neighbours, involving smashed windows, verbal abuse and intimidation.

Kim was becoming increasingly difficult to manage in her new primary school. She regularly ran out of school, sometimes going all the way home. Kim appeared isolated, caught in a bullying or victim cycle of interaction with her peers. Professionals shared concerns that Kim had been abused, although this had not been fully disclosed by either her mum or herself.

The special needs coordinator agreed that a Circle of Friends would be a useful approach for Kim. Colin was the educational psychologist and agreed to start up a circle for Kim. On the day of the whole-group session, Kim was running out of school even as Colin walked up the driveway. However, with some skilful coaxing from the staff who knew Kim well, she was persuaded to join the initial circle meeting following a very successful whole-group session.

Three meetings later, Kim's behaviour and relationships had visibly improved. The stealing and running away had apparently ceased. There had been no reports of bullying or victimisation. Colin left the first review meeting with reasons to feel extremely pleased with the early outcomes.

*Perseverance is needed*

One month later, on a visit to this school, Colin learned that Kim had been excluded. The Circle of Friends had abruptly ceased to run. The special needs coordinator was apologetic, but frustrated. The headteacher no longer felt able to provide cover for the class teacher who was supporting the circle on a week-by-week basis. The missing step here was that the headteacher had not been properly involved in committing to the process at the start. Inevitably, this step is crucial to the continuity of the work. Negotiations began again to get the circle up and running once more. The story continues ...

**Nicky's circle: A circle of learning support**

Nicky was a Year 5 (P6) pupil who had difficulties in using and understanding spoken language in the usual ways. As a result, he was often unsure what was expected of him in class and frequently the work he produced was below a level expected for someone of his age. Nicky excelled at sport and PE and gained the respect of his peers because of this. Staff felt Nicky was well liked by his classmates. He had received two hours' support each day from a classroom assistant for a number of years and it was Nicky's response to this support that was causing concern. Nicky had become increasingly reluctant to accept support and unwilling to attempt new learning tasks. He seemed to be losing all confidence in himself and in his ability as a learner. The only time he seemed happy was playing football in the playground.

Derek, the educational psychologist for Nicky's school, discussed with staff the idea of using a Circles of Friends approach to try to improve things. It was not immediately obvious how a circle could be helpful. After all, Nicky did not lack friendships and was popular. However, we felt that anything that could reduce Nicky's feelings of isolation in class might be helpful.

*A variation*

Some changes were needed to the key 'How would you feel? How would you act?' questions used in the initial whole-class session. We asked them to tell us how they felt and acted when they did not understand what they were supposed to be doing with a piece of classwork. These questions exposed a rich vein of pupil experience. Everyone readily identified with the 'when you don't know what to do' scenario. They knew the negative feelings this provoked and could tell us about the strategies they employed to deal with the situation, including going to the toilet for long periods, endlessly sharpening pencils, disappearing into the book corner and hoping not to be noticed, copying from neighbours and so on. It was a short step from this to identifying the things that others can do that are helpful to the person in this situation and this brainstorming gave us many ideas that were later shared with Nicky in the small group meeting.

Many of the things the circle members did for and with Nicky were low key and simple, just small acts of reassurance and confirmation in the course of a lesson. However, this circle got to the heart of the matter when they suggested that Nicky's support assistant should spend more time working with him in a small group rather than being with him by herself. Children know what makes them feel included and this circle was successful in doing this for Nicky. His attitude to work and his acceptance of support improved greatly as a result.

**Arundeep's circle: A snapshot of pupil perceptions**

Arundeep was a Year 3 (P4) pupil who had nearly been permanently excluded for aggression towards other pupils and staff in his inner-city primary school. Problems at home had fuelled an explosive temper and he had become isolated, friendless, disruptive in class and uncooperative. The following quotations indicate how a Circle of Friends helped Arundeep.

*Facilitator:*   What's changed since the group started at the beginning of term?

*Circle members:*   Lots of things.

*Facilitator:*   What are the positives?

*Circle members:*   He doesn't lose his temper now.
We trust him now.
He is picking his friends more wisely now.
His friends are closer now.
He does not answer back so much.
He has learned to say sorry.
He is closer to Jay [another pupil] now.

*Facilitator:*   What things are still issues you are working on?

*Circle members:*   He still needs to work on finishing his writing off.
He got sent in the hall for jumping on someone's back.

*Facilitator:*   What things have you done to support him?

*Circle members:*   We have created a chart for him. Five signatures mean he can sit on a chair at carpet time!
We give him more chances.
We have helped him to keep calm.
We have helped him with targets. For instance, if he doesn't shout, we reward him.
We have supported him so that he walks away from arguments with staff.
We try to prevent arguments.
We have talked him out of temper tantrums.
We have lent pencils to him to prevent arguments.

# Some final thoughts

Sometimes staff will judge that a whole-class session is not an appropriate starting point. This will usually be the case when the intended focus child already has a group of friends in Circle Two and the aim is to mobilise them to support him or her through a particular crisis, for example a serious illness or a significant bereavement.

In these kinds of situations, the facilitator can discuss with the focus pupil whom he or she would like to invite to be part of the circle of support and then make direct requests for help to those named. It can be useful as part of this process to ask the focus child to fill in the relationships diagram reproduced on p.62. This will help to clarify who is in this person's life and may be an important circle member.

Membership need not be confined to other pupils attending the same school. Indeed, anyone who has a close relationship and is willing to become involved is a potential circle member. Again, our advice is to be creative. Increasingly, we are trying to widen and strengthen circle membership and have successfully included people who do not usually figure in our planning meetings, such as the focus person's sister's boyfriend, the school caretaker, or a grandparent.

The message is that diverse voices provide diverse solutions to the difficulties being faced.

# Is there a theory to go with it?

This is primarily a workbook and values primer. It does not aim to explore the various theoretical constructs that can be used to go deeper into the psychological and social processes behind Circles of Friends work. None the less, it is worth looking at the further insights that are gained when circles work is viewed from a particular theoretical standpoint – *Social constructionism.*

Social constructionism is the name given to a relatively recent philosophical approach to the social sciences. The core construct of social constructionism is that the way we understand the world and ourselves is the result of the processes of interaction between groups of people. From this perspective, ideas only have meaning inasmuch as they are shared and agreed by others and the belief that there are universal truths which can be discovered by science and hold true for all time is rejected. Instead, what is seen to be true in a given place and time is a product of the social and historical context within which the ideas were developed and negotiated.

The key process by which ideas are given meaning by human societies is *narrative* – the stories we tell to make meanings. These stories are not viewed as simply the product of individual minds but are seen as being *created* in the shared space between the narrator and the audience. Thus there is a sense in which we do not know what we think until we attempt to relate this to others. Likewise, we gain our sense of what is *possible* (what can be constructed with others) through the act of narrating. If we take a social constructionist position, then by sharing stories we learn more about who we are and who we might become.

Circles of Friends provide a setting in which a social world can be created and, as a result, deeper understandings of one another are found.

'The problem' should not be seen as a deficit of some sort within the focus person, but should be viewed instead as a narrative that has grown up between the focus person and the key players in that person's life – classmates, teachers, family members and so on. The problem is something that all involved act out and the role of the focus person is to play his or her part in the story.

The 'dominant narrative' in the lives of people with disabilities will typically contain themes that emphasise dependency, developmental limitation, inability to contribute to society, lack of relationships or participation and a host of similarly constraining 'stories'. However, if we view these stories as socially mediated constructs rather than as evidence of underlying and immutable deficits, then it follows that action can be taken to rewrite the narrative and repair the stories in a way that is less costly to the focus person. This is possible because no *one* story ever encompasses all the feelings and experiences of the focus person. Less noticed parts of their interactions can be brought to the fore and woven into a fresh narrative.

**From theory to practice**

We would argue that this way of construing social action and what is therapeutic fits well with our experience of Circles of Friends in action. When a Circle of Friends is formed, the focus child is given a forum within which he or she can be supported in re-authoring the dominant narrative of his or her life. Members of the circle support this by contributing their knowledge of the 'less noticed' focus child and by acting in ways that help to bring these new parts of the narrative to life. Thus new aspects of the child are appreciated which no one had even noticed previously.

Notice also that, from this perspective, the story never ends, no one is 'cured' and life goes on in a more or less happy way depending on how well a new narrative can be created. As Jack Pearpoint often says, 'Inclusion is simple ... but it is not easy, we are given a lifetime to figure it out.'

**'Stories' and the reconstruction of disability**

A growing number of independent and self-supporting groups are forming in the UK and elsewhere to campaign for equality of opportunity for children and adults labelled disabled. One such group is the Sheffield-based 'Parents With Attitude' and readers are encouraged to get hold of their book *Let Our Children Be*. This book is subtitled *A collection of stories* and it is a deliberate attempt to reframe the lives and relationships of children with disabilities by publishing the narratives that are rarely heard – those of parents, siblings and friends of the disabled child.

Several of these narratives are hostile to the dominant (medical) narrative of disability with its emphasis on deficit and treatment. Many of the writers take care to emphasise how their lives and learning have been enriched by their experiences of being a parent of a child with a disability. This is in direct contradiction to the dominant narrative which only has stories of the 'burdens' carried by parents, their need for respite, the risk of marital breakdown and so on.

One of the aims of *Let Our Children Be* is to bring into being an alternative narrative of disability and, by so doing, let others know that they are not alone in what they might be thinking and to give them permission to see the world in other ways. In such ways is social reality constructed and in the field of disability there is a rich fund of powerful and life-enhancing stories waiting to be told.

> Why would you change him?
> Don't you realise that I can feel
> Your need to change him
> Your need for him to be other than as he is
> To be improved
> To be more or less or whatever
> You are disturbed by?
> Don't you understand that
> The comments you make about my child
> Tell about yourself
> And not about him?
> And the needs we discuss
> Are yours
> And not his
> When you look at my child

Jill Penman, *Let Our Children Be*

# Chapter 6

## Twelve frequently asked questions

In the past four years, we have made many in-service training presentations on inclusion and Circles of Friends. On most occasions, our audience has been practising teachers, educational psychologists or members of other LEA support services. This section contains a selection of the most common questions we have been asked and our evolving answers to them.

A note of caution is needed. The answers are our answers, not *the* answers or even your answers. We cannot know what will work best in your context, we can only say what has seemed to work in similar settings. It is for this reason that we urge you to be creative in how you apply the ideas in this book to the situation you are working in. As long as you have one eye fixed on the deeper values and principles behind Circles of Friends, you are free to find your own ways to build relationships and community in your workplace or family.

**Question 1**

*What if, at the end of the whole-class session, no one shows a willingness to be part of the focus child's circle?*

This is probably the most frequently voiced anxiety from anyone contemplating running the circles process. It is still experienced by those who have already run several successful sessions with different classes and tutor groups. Often this fear is fuelled by other adults around the child who may have experienced considerable frustration when trying to change the child's behaviour or when they have had to placate other pupils who have been made angry or fearful by the focus child. Our and many others' experience is that this fear is never realised if the facilitator has recruited the right people and asked the key questions from the heart, that is, as if they mattered.

Sometimes the whole-class session will be used by individual pupils as an opportunity to express their anger and frustration with the focus child. As long as the facilitator provides a boundary for these strong feelings and does not allow the session to become solely about complaining, it is helpful for this to happen – the message is that this is real and people are being listened to. With these feelings off their chests, the class is more likely to be able to move on and look at ways forward to help the focus child.

If, at the stage of enlisting support, things seem to be sluggish or uncertain, it is often helpful to put the recruitment issue back to the class by asking, 'Is there anyone who people think would be a helpful member of the circle and who hasn't yet come forward?' Groups always have suggestions when asked this and they are usually the right ones. The individuals nominated in this way usually agree!

**Question 2**

*What would you do with a child that smells? Surely you couldn't build a circle for them?*

The answer is: 'Build a Circle of Friends!' Friends are people who care enough to notice and tell the truth.

We like to put the answering of this question back to the person who asked it. Often hard questions like this are easier to think about and imagine solutions to if you personalise them. Therefore ask yourself: 'Who would tell you if you smelled?', 'Who would you be angry with for not telling you?', 'Who could you bear to hear this news from?'. These are answerable questions in a way that the anonymous 'What would you do with a child that smells?' is not. Put in a personal way, it is easier to think what you might do and therefore to have ideas for what could be done for the focus child. Another approach to answering this question is to remember that the person who smells may be aware of this but does not have a means of asking for help to overcome the problem. A Circle of Friends provides a context in which help can be sought.

**Question 3**

*I can think of at least seven children in my class who would benefit from this approach. Should I run circles for each of them?*

We doubt whether this would be manageable using the process we describe and likewise, we would not recommend that a circle has more than one focus child within it. However, we would recommend that readers get hold of a very useful paper by John Luckner, a professor of special education at the University of Northern Colorado (Luckner *et al.*, 1994). Here they will find a description of a personal and social education programme that was focused on a group of eight Year 5 and 6 pupils, all of whom were described as having difficulty in making and keeping friends.

This peer network included a child with a significant hearing loss about whom there were particular concerns regarding his lack of relationships within the class and the impact of his hearing loss on his chances of forming closer friendships. However, he was not the focus of the group's concerns. Each pupil in the group was asked to commit to attend the 'friendship sessions' for at least eight weeks. Luckner's paper describes the sequence of relationship-building activities that the group followed in their weekly meetings. The informal evaluations carried out at the end of the programme make it clear that there are many positive gains to be had from this low-key approach to relationship building. This piece of work also underlines the point that making and sustaining relationships is an area of tension for all pupils, not simply those labelled different or disabled.

**Question 4**

*What if a disclosure is made during the circle meeting?*

It is important, when briefing a new Circle of Friends, to ensure that all realise that they may be told something which they cannot keep secret or confidential. Pupils will need to be reminded that if they hear something important or worrying about or from the focus child, they should speak to an adult such as the teacher running the circle. It is quite possible that a disclosure could be made to an individual or within the group meeting itself. One of the strengths of the approach is that pupils learn to trust one another. Secrets and private sufferings have, in our and others' experience, been safely shared in the most successful circles.

**Question 5**

*What about circle members who become 'over-enthusiastic'?*

Some circle members quickly become very enthusiastic to support, befriend and bring about change in the focus pupil. Such enthusiasm may be very endearing to the facilitator or teacher attempting to set up a new circle, but clearly there are pitfalls to such enthusiasm. Disappointment, over-zealous watchfulness or leaving themselves vulnerable to bullying or violent outbursts or just being unable to cope with the focus child's needs are among some of these. Careful support, encouragement and guidance may be needed from the adult running the circle or indeed further frank and honest discussion between circle members about the issue may be helpful. The key message to the individual circle members is: *Never dive alone!*

Individuals within the circle should always be encouraged to work together and to avoid situations in which they may become vulnerable. Escorting a pupil home, visiting a pupil in his or her home, playing in an isolated area and so forth can be potentially dangerous for an individual pupil and they are much safer when there is more than one circle member involved in whatever activity is planned.

**Question 6**

*Can circles co-opt members?*

Yes. Stronger, older peers, relations, or even adults may at times be usefully co-opted into the circle and strengthen its work. Diversity brings strength and this is at the root of circle work. The right people who can make a difference to the individual need to be present. Sometimes the right person to co-opt is the one who is giving the circle most concerns because of his or her antagonism towards the focus child. A constructive way of viewing this antagonism is to say that this child also has an unmet need to belong. Inviting him or her to be part of the circle is a step towards meeting this need and will likely deal with the antagonism at the same time.

**Question 7**         *What other ways are there to encourage friendship?*

Just being with other children can be a critical variable in the development of friendships for the most vulnerable, especially those being educated in segregated settings. Mainstream classroom techniques to encourage friendships can include mentoring systems, peer tutoring, buddy schemes and cooperative learning groups (Luckner and McDonald, Teaming to Learn, *Perspectives on Deafness*, 10 (1), (1992)). Schools can encourage disabled and able-bodied pupils to get involved with other children in such extra-curricular activities as chess clubs, team sports, photography, and any variety of outdoor activities. Assemblies and lessons that focus on the importance of friendship and supportive relationships can helpfully be built in throughout the school curriculum.

Reading and discussing books about friendship, such as *Friends* by H. Heine, (MacMillan, 1985), is another straightforward way to promote the learning of friendship skills. Enrolling or inducting new pupils provides an excellent opportunity for teaching these skills. Discussion about pupils can focus on ways to help the newcomer feel welcome and secure. A welcoming committee can be formed or one or more class members can be assigned as *buddies* to help the new pupil adapt to classroom routines, the daily timetable and the physical geography of the school. Teachers should always be alert for opportunities to suggest meaningful interactions among pupils, building on their observations of children working together.

Teachers can arrange for pupils who need friends to work with more sociable classmates on activities such as cleaning blackboards, watering plants, carrying materials from car to school, or from room to room, running errands or returning books to the library. Within all of this, what are the key peer support skills we should focus on?

Luckner *et al.* (1994) provide an excellent response to this question as follows:

✔ Developing positive interactions: the skills of being positive, attentive, approving, encouraging and interested.

✔ Finding areas of compatibility: shared interests are the most common basis for friendship. Pupils need to understand the importance of expressing interest in the concerns and experiences of others, as well as their own.

✔ Empathising with others: learning to be understanding and sensitive to the concerns and feeling of others.

✔ Sharing and providing support: pupils need to learn to help, support and share with others, especially in times of need.

✔ Building trustworthiness and loyalty: pupils need to understand the concepts of honesty and loyalty as well as the specific behaviours that these require.

✔ Developing skills for conflict resolution: learning to protect one's own interests assertively without being either submissive or aggressive is a major challenge for both pupils and many adults.

**Question 8**     *What is the best way to choose circle members?*

This question is covered in Chapter 4. There are many ways in which a circle can be formed including the following:

✔ Random selection of pupils: Any random technique such as picking names from a hat can be used.

✔ Teacher selection: Teachers may wish to make their own selection of ideal circle members for the focus pupil. (We do not encourage this option as it can run the risk of old cycles of preference and selection taking precedence over other more important factors.)

✔ Facilitator selection: The facilitator makes the choice on the basis of contributions to the whole-class session. (We do not prefer this method as a silent member of the whole-group session may hold an essential key to relationships with the focus pupil.)

✔ Pupil selection: The class or tutor group simply nominate a number of pupils who they feel to be best suited to support the focus pupil. They can be prompted to consider shared interests, hobbies or other activities or to consider other strengths of fellow classmates including strong personality, communication skills, negotiation skills, popularity and, most importantly, street credibility.

✔ A compromise involving facilitator, teacher and pupil selection: The facilitator and the teacher each choose two members on the basis of their knowledge of the class or tutor group and the pupils choose the rest. At the time of writing, this is the method of selection we are using most often. But remember – what works best for us may not be best for you.

✔ The focus pupil selects members of his or her circle from volunteers: The focus pupil is given the names of volunteers and is asked to suggest other names of pupils who would be most helpful, supportive and usefully challenging within his or her Circle of Friends. This would provide maximum control to the focus pupil and strengthen his or her ownership but would also contain some disadvantages. There is a security and a sense of clear boundaries for a focus pupil who is able to meet an already formed circle where all have volunteered and have been selected using methods drawn from the above list.

**Question 9**

*How long do children need to remain as members of the circle?*

We have already stressed the need for the facilitator to provide boundaries for the circle members in order to allow safe expression of feelings. Time boundaries are also important and it can be helpful to let prospective circle members know that their commitment will be expected for a set period (a school term is a useful block of time) and that after this, they will have the choice of continuing for a further period or of opting out for a spell. In practice, we have found that opting out is rare in successful circles: however, circle members find it reassuring to know that they can.

**Question 10**

*Can the circle meet without the focus child present?*

Strictly speaking, this is not an option that has any place in an authentic approach to Circles of Friends work. The circle is built around the focus child who must have the final say on decisions taken and the power to influence how things are viewed by others. This is unlikely to be possible if he or she is not at the meeting.

In practice, much will depend on the skills of the facilitator and his or her ability to enable difficult issues and individual circle members' frustrations to be aired in a constructive way. Some facilitators have felt the need to convene a circle meeting without the focus child present. This has usually occurred when things appear to be going badly, and the efforts of circle members are felt to be having little effect on identified issues and it is felt that they would benefit from a chance to offload some of their frustrations. This may be a helpful step to take if the alternative is the collapse of the circle, but if you are finding that you are having frequent circle meetings without the focus child, you have strayed way off track and are no longer facilitating a Circle of Friends.

**Question 11**          *What if it all goes wrong?*

This work does involve risks. Human relationships involve risks. But the risks of doing nothing or of staying with tried and tested methods are much greater. Remember, Circles of Friends can actually stop children being excluded or segregated. Particular risks in school settings that are worth being aware of, when using Circles of Friends, include the following:

✔ *Sabotage*. This may be caused by senior members of staff or by colleagues and has a variety of motivations. Sabotage can occur in all innocence as a result of chaotic planning, or can arise from a lack of understanding of the Circles of Friends process.

✔ *Continuity breaks*. Things can get off track when circle meetings are brought to an untimely end due to cover problems, staff absence or the work not being seen as high priority. This breaks the flow and commitment of the circle and is particularly unhelpful to the focus pupil.

✔ *Feelings of exclusion*. Other members of staff may be unwittingly threatened by the relationship you have formed with the focus child and his or her circle. They may feel deskilled by the enthusiasm you have created or resentful of the time you have found or negotiated for your work with the circle. Whatever triggers these feelings, the associated behaviours can be potentially destructive. Beware.

✔ *Over-enthusiasm*. This can lead to individual circle members placing themselves in high-risk situations with the focus pupil. Individuals always need reminding to work together in mutual support rather than going it alone.

✔ *Parental anxiety*. Parents of the focus pupil or parents of members of the circle may become unduly anxious about the Circles of Friends work. This usually occurs where parents have not been properly informed about what is happening or are relying on rumour, or reacting to a particular event.

At other times, if you are not confident or comfortable with the direction in which things are going, you will have the option of having further consultations with whoever provided the initial external facilitation. When things get difficult, it is often because the circle has been over-ambitious in its early planning and its expectations of being able to make a difference. Try to simplify and reduce the number of aims being worked towards. Assess the risks within your own situation and plan your action accordingly. This work is worth the risk! You should always aim to work together with another person, possibly a colleague, and always ensure that individuals in the key positions within your school setting fully understand and support what you are trying to do.

Never go it alone!

**Question 12**        *What if ... ?*

This is the last question, and it is not really a frequently *asked* question but it may be a frequently *thought* question. If there is an answer, it is that sometimes we have *no idea* what the way forward is. This answer is a counsel against the culture of professionalism that implies that every situation is covered and every question has an answer if only we knew who we should refer to. To be able to say with honesty that you don't know what to do next is often a therapeutic thing to do. It passes the power back to the person that is seeking help.

# APPENDIX A:   USEFUL HANDOUTS

## TRACKING DOCUMENT

**Circles of Friends for:**

Date:

Name of circle:

Pupils present:



Meeting place:                                Review date:

| **Positives** | **Issues** |
|---|---|
| | |

**Discussion points:**

**Agreed action:**

Signed:

# REVIEW

## Circles of Friends for:

Facilitated by:

Outside facilitator:

Date:

Name of circle:                                    Circle started on:

Meeting place:                                     Who was present at review?

Names of pupils involved in circle:

Were any circle meetings cancelled?      Reason:

Attendance at meetings?

Full          Partial

### Behaviour changes reported by:

| Staff | Parents | Pupils | Circle pupils |
|-------|---------|--------|---------------|
|       |         |        |               |
|       |         |        |               |
|       |         |        |               |
|       |         |        |               |
|       |         |        |               |

**Positives of approach:**                     **Emerging issues:**

**Future action:**

# AN INTRODUCTION TO CIRCLES OF FRIENDS

## A staff guide

These brief notes will give you some background information and an idea of what would be entailed in setting up and running a Circle of Friends in your school.

1.  Circles of Friends originated in North America as one of a range of strategies to encourage the inclusion of children with disabilities into mainstream settings. Circles have been used to support children with a wide range of disabilities and have also been used in the community. The approach has been developed in Nottingham, Bristol and elsewhere in the UK and has been shown to be very effective.

2.  A circle usually consists of 6–8 volunteers (most often from the same class or tutor group) who meet regularly (usually weekly) with the 'focus child' and an adult. The circle has three main tasks: to offer encouragement and recognition for successes and progress; to identify difficulties, set targets and devise strategies for achieving targets; and to help to put these ideas into practice.

3.  Setting up a circle includes the following steps:

    ✔ Gaining the support and agreement of the focus child and his or her parents.

    ✔ A meeting with the whole class (which the focus child does not attend) aimed at identifying those willing to be supporters, which takes roughly 30–40 minutes.

    ✔ Informing the parents of those chosen to be circle members and gaining their agreement to their children's participation.

    ✔ Weekly meetings of the circle, the focus child, and an adult facilitator (taking 20–30 minutes).

# AN INTRODUCTION TO CIRCLES OF FRIENDS

## A parents' guide

### 1. What is a Circle of Friends?

A circle is a group of 6–8 youngsters who have volunteered to meet regularly with your child and a teacher (usually this is for 20–30 minutes per week).

### 2. What is a Circle for and what happens?

The circle has four main aims:

- ✔ To create a support network of other pupils for your child.
- ✔ To help your child cope more easily in school and give him or her more choices.
- ✔ To provide your child with encouragement and recognition for any achievements and progress.
- ✔ To work with your child in identifying difficulties and coming up with practical ideas to help to sort these out.

The adult is there to help the circle, but the youngsters do the work with your child – coming up with ideas, trying things out, reporting back.

The circle can't provide instant friendship – but we hope that it will help your child to build closer and better connections and relationships with other children.

### 3. How will it be set up?

The members of your child's class would be asked if they are interested in being part of the circle. Your child's teacher will explain to them what this involves – usually this is best done when your child is not actually in the room.

We almost always end up with more pupils who are willing to help than we need and your child's class teacher will be involved in selection along with other class members. The group then meets regularly with an adult.

### 4. Will it help?

Obviously we can't guarantee this. However, Circles of Friends has been used quite widely in Canada, America and increasingly in this country. Evaluations in this country have so far been very positive and have helped children who have had complex difficulties and disabilities:

- ✔ Children at the centre of the circles have often shown improved behaviour and less worry about mixing with their classmates.
- ✔ The volunteers have been very good at coming up with creative and practical ideas.
- ✔ Most volunteers have been keen to continue their involvement.
- ✔ School staff have found the circles to be very worthwhile.

Please contact . . . . . . . . . . . . . . . . . . . . . . if you would like to discuss 'Circles' in more detail or if you have any questions or concerns.

# A LETTER TO PARENTS OF VOLUNTEERS

Dear

The school has become involved in a project to set up and run what are called Circles of Friends. These are made up of 6 to 8 children who have agreed to help one of their classmates. Usually the Circles help someone to get on with other children. It involves the group in meeting once a week for 20–30 minutes (during lunchtime) with a teacher and the focus child to come up with solutions and ideas for sorting out any difficulties.

The idea is being used in other parts of the country. As well as helping the focus child, it has been found to have benefits for all the young people in the Circle. In particular, it seems to help them to develop their ability to think through problems and helps with their understanding of themselves and others.

<Child's name> has agreed to be part of the Circle (though of course may opt out after an agreed time). We are very grateful for <child's name>'s willingness to become involved and we hope that you are happy with this. If you have any concerns or questions, please let us know as soon as possible.

# THE WHOLE-CLASS MEETING – RECRUITING VOLUNTEERS

1. **Introduction**
   a) Explain your involvement with focus child.
   b) Explain your interest in how youngsters get on with and can help each other.

2. **Ground rules**
   a) Treat each other with respect.
   b) Listen … one person speaking at a time.
   c) Confidentiality.

3. **Need to talk about focus pupil**
   a) Emphasise this is unusual (to talk behind someone's back).
   b) Focus pupil knows this is happening.
   c) Reason is that you need their help to think about ways in which focus pupil can be helped (stress need for/ value of their insights).

4. **Need for confidentiality (explain)**
   a) No reference to who said what about whom – the details stay in this class.
   b) Emphasise that this confidentiality also binds adults.

5. **Listing positives**
   a) Focus on positives first – good at …, nice things about …, what the focus child does well.
   b) List all contributions on a flip chart.

6. **Where things do not go so well/ difficult times for focus child**
   a) Explain that you've heard about some difficulties, but probably not all.
   b) Ask for descriptions of behaviour – list.
   c) Describe sort of person he or she is – list.

7. **Discussion of friendships**
   a) Display circle diagram (p.62) and introduce the circles:
      i) People you love and who love you
      ii) Allies/best friends
      iii) Friends/acquaintances
      iv) People paid to be in your life.
   b) Fill in a volunteer's circles on the flip chart with help from class.
   c) All fill in own circle diagram privately.

8. **What would it be like if …**
   a) What would it be like if Circles 2 and 3 had no people in them?
   b) How would it feel? – make a list.
   c) How would they behave? – make a list. Compare to flip chart from 6.

9. **List ideas to support focus child: enlist empathy, support and commitment**

10. **What's involved**
    a) Explain about the idea of Circles of Friends and that you want to set up a group which will help with <child's name>'s difficulties.
    b) Explain what would be required, e.g. meeting at lunchtime once a week.
    c) Explain that only six to eight will be involved.
    d) Pass out small pieces of paper. Ask them to think about whether they would like to volunteer, then to write their name on the paper with *either* a yes or a no. Stress confidentiality and 'no pressure'.
    e) Explain that not everyone will be able to do it *but*
       i) may need new people in group at later date.
       ii) everyone can take responsibility for helping.
       iii) letter home to all parents of those chosen, explaining about it.

# THE FIRST MEETING OF THE CIRCLE

1. Introductions.

2. Restate ground rules.

   a) Listen to each other.
   b) Treat each other as we would like to be treated.

3. Reminder of the aims.

   a) To work with <child's name> to help him or her make friends.
   b) To help him or her identify and sort out difficulties.
   c) To support each other in helping <child's name>.

4. Ask each to state reason for wanting to be in group.

5. Ask group to list positives (point out that <child's name> didn't hear what was said at first session). Ask <child's name> to add any to list.

6. Ask group to list situations where things do not go so well and what <child's name> needs to work on.

   a) Ask for descriptions of behaviours.
   b) Turn each problem behaviour into a positive target (describing what <child's name> should be doing rather than *not* doing).
   c) Ask <child's name> to add to any of lists a) or b).
   d) Talk about what would be different if <child's name> achieved these targets – for him or her and for others.

7. Introduce problem-solving.

   a) Explain need to work on one or two targets at a time.
   b) Ask group to decide which target(s) (including <child's name> in discussion). Suggest that it may be best to start with something quickly achievable.
   c) Brainstorm possible ways to get to the target.
   d) Select jointly and help group spell out steps.
   e) Agree responsibilities and boundaries (emphasise that <child's name> is responsible for own behaviour).
   f) Emphasise realism about speed of change, setbacks, etc.

8. Agree name for group.

9. Arrange next meeting.

# SUBSEQUENT MEETINGS OF THE CIRCLE

1.  **Warm-up/settling-in exercise**

2.  **Good news**

    a)  Ask for any situation involving <child's name> which went well
        (involving or witnessed by the members)

        i)   Get detail as to what <child's name> said or did.
        ii)  Explore how participants felt.

    b)  Ask for any success in working towards targets.

3.  **Bad news**

    a)  Discuss any blockages in steps towards target.
    b)  Brainstorm solutions.
    c)  Any other problems.

4.  **Target setting**

    a)  Maybe more of same, different means to same end, or a new target.
    b)  Brainstorm solutions (if not already done in 3b).
    c)  Plan detail and agree responsibility and action.

# RELATIONSHIPS DIAGRAM
## Concentric circles

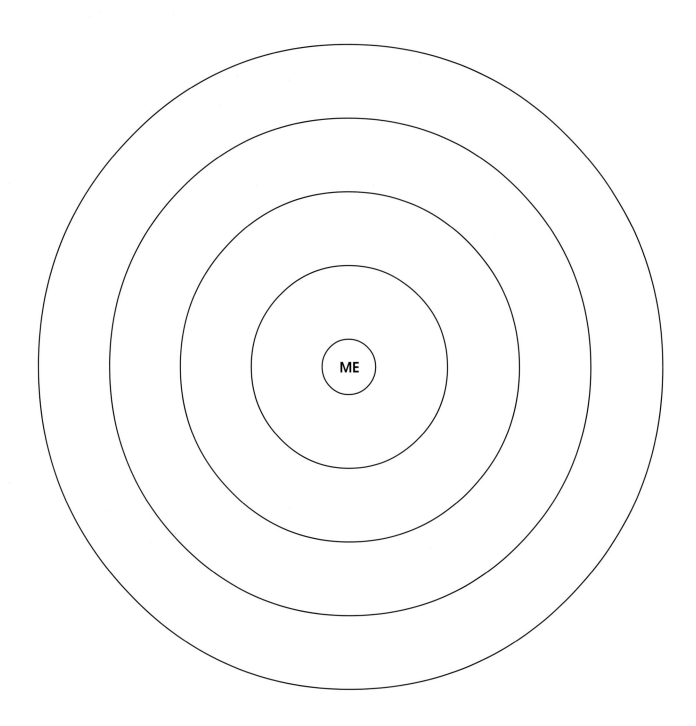

# APPENDIX B:  RESOURCES

This section contains references, organisations and resources relating to the vision and practice of inclusion and, in particular, to work with Circles of Friends or support. Some of the materials referenced can only be obtained in the UK through Inclusion Distribution, the UK outlet for Inclusion Press. We have also included some websites that we think are worth a visit.

**References**

Falvey, M. A., Forest, M., Pearpoint, J. and Rosenberg, R., *All My Life's a Circle – Using the Tools: Circles, Maps and Path* (Inclusion Press, 1994)

Gray, C. A. and Garand, J. D., Social stories: Improving responses of students with autism with accurate social information, *Focus on Autistic Behaviour*, 8 (1), (1993)

Hanko, G., *Special Needs in Ordinary Classrooms – From Staff Development to Staff Support*, 3rd ed. (David Fulton Publishers, 1995)

Jordan, L. and Goodey, C., *Human Rights and School Change – The Newham Story* (The Centre for Studies in Inclusive Education, Bristol, 1996)

Lovett, H., *Learning to Listen: Positive Approaches and People with Difficult Behaviour* (Jessica Kingsley, 1996)

Luckner, J., Schauermann, D., and Allen, R., Learning to be a friend, *Perpectives on Deafness*, 12 (5), (1994)

McLeod, J., *Narrative and Psychotherapy* (Sage Publications, 1997)

Mosley, J., *Quality Circle Time in the Primary Classroom* (LDA, 1996)

Murray, P. and Penman, J., *Let Our Children Be. A Collection of Stories* (Parents with Attitude, c/o 44 Cowlishaw Road, Sheffield S11 8XF, 1996)

Newton, C. and Tarrant, T., *Managing Change in Schools* (Routledge, 1992)

Pearpoint, J., Forest, M. and Snow, J., *The Inclusion Papers – Strategies to Make Inclusion Work* (Inclusion Press, 1993)

Perske, R. and Perske, M., *Circles of Friends* (Abingdon Press, 1988)

Shaw, L., *Each Belongs – Integrated Education in Canada* (The Centre for Studies in Inclusive Education, Bristol, 1990)

Snow, J., *What's Really Worth Doing and How to Do it* (Inclusion Press, 1994)

Thomas, G., Inclusive schools for an inclusive society, *British Journal of Special Education*, 24 (3), (1997)

Villa, R. A. and Thousand, J. S., *Creating an Inclusive School* (Paul H. Brookes Publishing, 1995)

Wertheimer, A., *Circles of Support – Building Inclusive Communities* (Circles Network, Bristol, 1995)

Whitaker, P., Barratt, P., Joy, H., Potter, M. and Thomas, G., Children with autism and peer group support: Using circles of friends, *British Journal of Special Education* (1998)

Books and videos published or produced by Inclusion Press are available in the UK from Inclusion Distribution, 29 Heron Drive, Poynton, Stockport SK12 1QR Tel: 01625 859146

The Alliance for Inclusive Education can be contacted at Unit 2, 70 South Lambeth Road, London SW8 1RL   Tel: 0171 735 5277

Circles Network can be contacted through Mandy Neville, Director, Circles Network, Pamwell House, 160 Pennywell Road, Upper Easton, Bristol BS5 0TX Tel: 0117 939 3917

**Video material**

*With a Little Help from my Friends* available from Inclusion Distribution.

*Altogether Better* by Richard Rieser and Micheline Mason available from Comic Relief Education, Unit 2, Drywall Estate, Castle Road, Sittingbourne, Kent ME10 3RL.

*Kids Belong Together* available from Inclusion Distribution.

*Circles of Support* – the companion video to the book *Circles of Support – Building Inclusive Communities* available from Circles Network.

*NEW MAPS Training Video Shafik's Map* (plus ... *'Dreaming'* **with Judith Snow**) available from Inclusion Distribution.

**Websites on the Internet**

*http://inclusion.com*
Links to other websites dealing with inclusion and lists resources produced by Inclusion Press.

*http://www.lsi.ukans.edu/beach/beachhp.htm*
Training and dissemination activities to aid inclusion of children with disabilities.

*http://www.asri.edu/CFSP*
Assistance to those developing inclusive educational and community supports.

*http://www.grove.com/*
The leading authority on graphic facilitation and other process tools.

*http://funrsc.fairfield.edu/~jfleitas/contkids.html*
Issues relating to children with chronic medical conditions at school.

*http://www.downsyndrome.com*
Practical approaches to inclusion of pupils with disabilities in mainstream schools.

*http://www.mailbase.ac.uk/lists-p-t/senco-forum/welcome.html*
Active debates on current special needs issues.

*http://www.innotts.co.uk/~colinn/epsweb.htm*
The authors' website. Links to a number of the above sites and others of interest.

*http://www.oise.on.ca/~bwillard/facinfo.htm*
Ideas and links relevant to facilitation skills and process tools.

*http://soeweb.syr.edu/thechp/hppress.htm*
A policy, research and advocacy organisation for the rights of the disabled.

*http://www.kidstogether.org/*
Information and resources that improve the quality of life for the disabled.

*http://www.iod.unh.edu/projects/isd.htm*
Abstracts of research on the practice of inclusion in education.

*http://ep.open.ac.uk/wgma/CSIE/csiehome.html*
The major UK source of information and advice on inclusive education.

CAMPAIGN 352

# DETTINGEN 1743

Miracle on the Main

**MICHAEL MCNALLY**

ILLUSTRATED BY SEÁN Ó'BRÓGÁIN

*Series editor Marcus Cowper*

OSPREY PUBLISHING
Bloomsbury Publishing Plc
PO Box 883, Oxford, OX1 9PL, UK
1385 Broadway, 5th Floor, New York, NY 10018, USA
E-mail: info@ospreypublishing.com
**www.ospreypublishing.com**

OSPREY is a trademark of Osprey Publishing Ltd

First published in Great Britain in 2020

A catalogue record for this book is available from the British Library.

ISBN: PB 9781472836809; eBook 9781472836816; ePDF 9781472836786;
XML 9781472836793

20 21 22 23 24   10 9 8 7 6 5 4 3 2 1

Maps by www.bounford.com
3D BEVs by Paul Kime
Index by Zoe Ross
Typeset by PDQ Digital Media Solutions, Bungay, UK
Printed and bound in India by Replika Press Private Ltd.

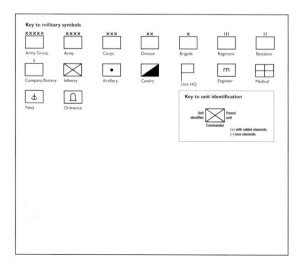

## Artist's note

Readers may care to note that the original paintings from which the colour
plates in this book were prepared are available for private sale. All
reproduction copyright whatsoever is retained by the publishers. All
enquiries should be addressed to:

seanobrogain@yahoo.ie

The publishers regret that they can enter into no correspondence upon
this matter.

Osprey Publishing supports the Woodland Trust, the UK's leading woodland
conservation charity.

To find out more about our authors and books visit
**www.ospreypublishing.com**. Here you will find extracts, author
interviews, details of forthcoming events and the option to sign up for
our newsletter.

## Author's acknowledgements

As always there is a group of 'go-to' friends and collaborators when it comes
to discussing theories, word-flow or even travelling to a battlefield to get a
'feel' for the terrain. I would therefore like to thank (in no specific order)
Andy Copestake, Jurrien de Jong, Robert Hall, Michel Hanotaux, Seán
Ó'Brogáin, Iain Stanford and David Wilson.

I also wish to thank M. Charles Deligne of the Musée d'Histoire Militaire
(Military History Museum), Tournai for permitting the use of several images
in this work. The museum is located at Rue Roc Saint-Nicaise 59-61, 7500
Tournai, Belgium, and contains numerous rooms dedicated to Tournai's
military history from 1100 up to 1945.

I would also like to thank Gabriele Mendella, whose stunning period
dress recreations can be seen throughout this work. Readers can find out
more about Gabriele's work by visiting: www.facebook.com/
LaMaisonDuRoy

This title – my tenth for Osprey – sees a parting of the ways after some
15 years. Again, I would like to offer my thanks and gratitude both to
Marcus Cowper, my long-suffering editor, for his friendship, guidance and
wisdom over the years, and also to Nikolai Bogdanovic, who will be picking
up the baton, as it were. Towards the end of the book you'll see, I hope,
how apt an analogy that is.

Finally, my greatest thanks go to four people to whom I owe the greatest
debt and without whose support none of this would be possible – my wife
Petra, and children Stephen, Elena-Rose and Liam Patrick Sean – you are
the reason that makes it all worthwhile.

## Dedication

It gives me great pleasure to dedicate this book to Franz Biller and Helmut
Winter of the Geschichtsverein Karlstein am Main, both for their kindness
and hospitality during my visits to the battlefield, and for their graciousness
in allowing me access to archival material on the battle. Without their
support, this volume would be greatly different from the one that you are
reading – *Ein tiefes und Herzliches "Dankeschön" an euch beide.*

## A note on images

Unless otherwise indicated, the images that appear in this work are from
the author's collection.

**PREVIOUS PAGE**
King George II of Great Britain at the Battle of Dettingen.

# CONTENTS

# The Hapsburg patrimony upon the death of Charles VI

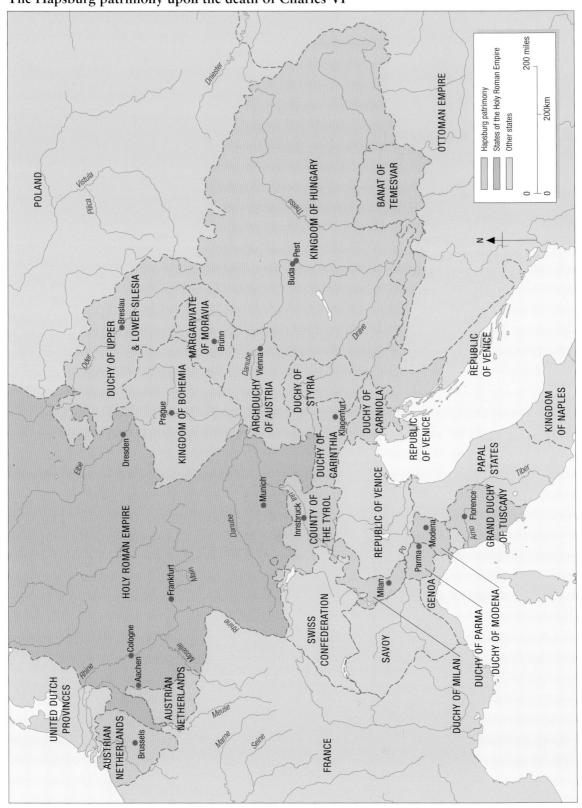

# ORIGINS OF THE CAMPAIGN

Beginning with a dynastic dispute, and ending with the destruction of a ruling house, the 18th century was a period of history in which cultural developments were punctuated by no fewer than 23 wars and conflicts, some of which lasted for months and others for years. Of these, no fewer than five were fought to decide who should rule over a given territory.

In 1701, a dubious and disputed deathbed testimony had led to rival coalitions seeking to place their chosen candidate upon the throne of Spain. The late king – Charles II – had been a member of the Spanish branch of the House of Hapsburg, and without any direct male heir, it was naturally believed that he would be succeeded by a member of the Austrian branch of the family. However, as Charles lay dying, he apparently changed his will, bequeathing his throne to a French-sponsored candidate, possibly on the grounds that King Louis XIV of France was descended from the Hapsburgs on his mother's side, but also, and perhaps of more direct relevance, because France shared a natural border with Spain and could easily send troops across the Pyrenees to press her claim.

A problematic situation was rendered more so with the fact that both Louis XIV and his cousin Leopold I, the Holy Roman Emperor and head of the Austrian Hapsburgs, had married two of Charles' elder sisters, and crucially, it was the French queen – as the elder of the two and the only issue from their father's first marriage – who had the better claim to the succession.

As always, the solution was not a straightforward one, as it was also stipulated that neither of the contenders, nor their direct heirs, could personally inherit the Spanish crown, a measure designed to prevent a direct union of the kingdoms. There was, however, nothing to prevent the accession of a second or even a third son. Both sides therefore began to canvass for allies, the Austrians in support of the Archduke Charles von Hapsburg (Leopold's second son from his third marriage), whilst the French mobilized their adherents behind King Louis' second grandson, Philippe, Duke of Anjou.

In July 1701, open warfare broke out, but in the spring of 1711, one of the principal catalysts for the conflict

Charles VI, Holy Roman Emperor. It was his political manoeuvring in order to secure the Austrian succession for his own children that plunged Europe into a war lasting almost eight years.

Charles Albert, Electoral Prince of Bavaria, and subsequently Holy Roman Emperor as Charles VII. He would gain his heart's desire, but not live long enough to establish a ruling dynasty.

Maria Theresia, Empress Consort, Archduchess of Austria, Queen of Hungary. It was to her that the task of protecting the legacy of her father, Charles VI, would fall.

was dramatically removed from the playing board. On 17 April, Joseph I – who had succeeded as Holy Roman Emperor in 1705 – contracted smallpox and died. As the father of two daughters, his designated heir was his younger brother (Charles von Hapsburg), who, at that time, was vying for the Spanish crown. Upon his acceptance of the imperial dignity, Charles immediately removed himself as a candidate for the Spanish throne, and thus – to all intents and purposes – the War of the Spanish Succession was over: it was now up to the politicians to resolve a diplomatic settlement.

But even as one war reached its conclusion, the seeds of a future conflict were being sown. Before the death of their father, Leopold's two sons had signed the Mutual Pact of Succession, by which should Charles succeed as emperor but fail to have a male heir, the succession to the Hapsburg lands would revert to Joseph's two daughters: Maria Josepha (b.1699) and Maria Amalia (b.1701). Determined that his line would continue to rule, and despite the fact that he was at that time childless, Charles VI began a diplomatic odyssey by which he sought to gain support amongst the crowned heads of Europe for any as yet unborn daughter to succeed him in the event of his having no direct male heir. In effect, and despite the agreement with his brother, the new emperor was making a clear and conscious effort to disinherit his two nieces, neither of whom would be permitted to marry unless they first renounced all claims to the Hapsburg patrimony.

In April 1716, the succession seemed to be assured with the birth of the Archduke Leopold Johann. However, the young prince died during the winter, and imperial hopes would now rest with the Archduchess Maria Theresia, who was born in May of the following year. The emperor's designs had seemingly borne fruit – for his lifetime at least – with the acceptance of his compact, by now referred to as the Pragmatic Sanction, not only by the member states of the Holy Roman Empire, but also by countries such as Great Britain, France and Spain. Any ensuing political harmony was a short-lived affair, as, having obeyed their uncle and renounced their claims to the Hapsburg patrimony, the archduchesses Maria Josepha and Maria Amalia were soon married, the former to Frederick Augustus, Crown Prince of Saxony, and the latter to Charles Albert, Electoral Prince of Bavaria, two men who by virtue of birth had as much claim to the imperial throne as Emperor Charles VI himself.

Although the emperor was sitting on a political powder keg of his own creation, it was to be his former rival the Duke of Anjou, now King Philip V of Spain, who would upset the European status quo by attempting to recover Spain's Italian territories that had been ceded at the end of the War of the Spanish Succession. Initially, the war went well for Spain, but as her successes mounted, so did opposition to her aggression. France, Great Britain, Austria and the United Dutch Provinces eventually signed the Quadruple Alliance, and with the strongest powers in Europe now ranged against her, the government in Madrid had little option other than to seek terms and capitulate.

With the Spanish defeat, a cloak of normality and peace now descended over Europe. However, it was not long before the armies were again mobilized, this time following the death – in 1733 – of the Elector Frederick Augustus of Saxony who, from 1697 to 1706 and then 1709 to 1733, had also ruled Poland as King Augustus II. The Bourbon powers of France and Spain threw their weight behind Stanislaus Leszczyński, King Louis XV's father-in-law, whilst Austria and Russia supported the newly elevated Electoral Prince of Saxony, Frederick Augustus II, husband of the Archduchess Maria Josepha, the former undoubtedly hoping to cement Saxon support for the Pragmatic Sanction. For their part, Great Britain and the United Dutch Provinces chose to adopt a position of strict neutrality, and although the Imperial Diet was to pass a resolution declaring a state of war between the Holy Roman Empire and France, this would be largely negated by the intrigues of the Elector Charles Albert of Bavaria, husband of the Archduchess Maria Amalia, who had already received a tacit promise of French support in the event of his ever making a bid for the imperial throne. By 1735, the war had all but petered out, having resulted in a victory for Frederick Augustus and his allies, but it would not be until 1738 that a formal peace treaty was signed; Leszczyński, having renounced all claims to the Polish crown, was compensated with the Duchy of Lorraine, whose ruler, Francis Stephen, husband of the Archduchess Maria Theresia, was instead granted the Grand Duchy of Tuscany in Italy. For her part, France once again reiterated her support for the Pragmatic Sanction.

For Emperor Charles VI, time was running out, and two years after this last diplomatic success, he died in Vienna on 20 October 1740, the dogged pursuit of his posterity having driven the Austrian state into a position of almost total bankruptcy. If Charles had died satisfied with his apparent political success, his heiress was soon to be disabused of any such illusions, as, within weeks of her father's death, Bavaria, France, Prussia, Spain and Saxony-Poland would all renounce their previous agreements. If Maria Theresia wished to succeed her father, she would need to fight for her right to do so.

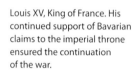

Louis XV, King of France. His continued support of Bavarian claims to the imperial throne ensured the continuation of the war.

A French infantryman's sword. Note the fleur-de-lis engraved upon the blade. (Reproduced with courtesy and with kind permission of Musée d'Histoire Militaire, Tournai)

# THE IMPERIAL ELECTION OF 1742

Although hostilities had begun with a pre-emptive Prussian attack on the Austrian province of Silesia in December 1740 coupled with a Franco-Bavarian drive upon Prague, much of 1741 would be given over to the politicking and jockeying for the upcoming imperial election, which would not only approve Charles VI's successor as Holy Roman Emperor but could also, depending on the result of the election, provide a figurehead who would enforce a peace settlement and bring hostilities to an end.

In February 1742, and as protocol demanded, the representatives of the nine imperial electors went into conclave at Frankfurt to debate the

A British grenadier's sabre. The running fox or wolf may denote that this weapon was made at Shotley Bridge, Birmingham. (Reproduced with courtesy and kind permission of Musée d'Histoire Militaire, Tournai)

candidatures of the two men who had chosen to stand for the highest imperial office: Francis Stephen of Lorraine, and Charles Albert of Bavaria. After the first round of voting, Francis had received four nominations, namely that of Bohemia (his wife, Maria Theresia), Brunswick-Lüneburg (George II of Great Britain and Hanover), Mainz (Philipp Karl von Eltz-Kempenich) and Trier (Georg von Schönborn); whilst Charles had only received the votes of Bavaria (himself), Cologne (his brother Clemens August) and the Palatinate (his cousin Charles Philip). The remaining two electorates – Brandenburg and Saxony – remained uncommitted to either party.

With a majority of 4:3 in his favour, it seemed certain that Francis Stephen would win the election, but behind the scenes France now began to put diplomatic and financial pressure upon the two abstainers in favour of her preferred candidate. Charles then dropped a diplomatic bombshell by announcing that the participation of Maria Theresia in the election had been invalid, arguing that the crown of Bohemia was electoral and not hereditary, and that as he himself had been crowned king when the Franco-Bavarian forces had captured Prague, he was the legitimate possessor of the Bohemian vote, which would naturally be cast in his favour.

Continuing, he added that even if the electoral college chose to disagree with his assertion, the Pragmatic Sanction still remained a flawed and disputed agreement, as it could not be held to supersede the Mutual Pact of Succession. Thus, he concluded, as the daughters of the elder brother (Joseph I), both his wife and that of the Elector of Saxony had a far better claim to any part of the Hapsburg patrimony than the daughter of Charles VI.

Combined with French actions behind the scenes, it proved to be a telling argument, with the Bohemian vote now being declared invalid, and the electors of Brandenburg and Saxony (who were both currently at war with Austria) falling into line behind Bavaria, Cologne and the Palatinate. Thus, with five votes for, three against and one invalid vote, the Bavarian elector was crowned as Emperor Charles VII, the first non-Hapsburg emperor in almost three centuries.

# CHRONOLOGY

| | |
|---|---|
| 1697 | 7 April: birth of Charles Albert von Wittelsbach, Electoral Prince of Bavaria, and from 24 January 1742 until 20 January 1745 Holy Roman Emperor. |
| 1713 | 19 April: promulgation of the Pragmatic Sanction, a legal device to facilitate the succession to the Hapsburg hereditary possessions through the female line. |
| 1717 | 17 May: birth of Archduchess Maria Theresia von Hapsburg, later Queen of Hungary and Holy Roman Empress (Consort). |
| 1734–35 | War of the Polish Succession. Peace is not finalized, however, until 1738. |
| 1735 | France endorses the Pragmatic Sanction. |
| 1735–39 | Russo-Turkish War. |
| 1738 | France renounces the Pragmatic Sanction and offers support to Charles Albert of Bavaria in any future imperial elections. |

## 1740

| | |
|---|---|
| 20 October | Death of Charles VI (von Hapsburg), Holy Roman Emperor. |
| 16 December | Frederick of Prussia renounces the Pragmatic Sanction and Prussian forces invade the Austrian province of Silesia. |

## 1741

| | |
|---|---|
| 10 April | Prussians defeat Austrians at Mollwitz. |
| 5 June | First Treaty of Breslau signed between France and Prussia. |
| 15 August | French forces under François-Marie de Broglie cross the Rhine and unite with Bavarian forces in upper Austria. |
| September | Maria Theresia appeals to the Hungarian Diet for support; Hungarians agree to provide an 'Insurrectio' or levy-en-masse of 60,000 men. Defensive agreement signed between Austria and Hanover. |
| 9 October | Austrian forces under Wilhelm Reinhard von Neipperg abandon Silesia in order to counter the threat to Vienna. |
| 9 December | Following the capture of Prague by French forces, Charles Albert is crowned King of Bohemia, claiming the kingdom's vote in the imperial elections (hereto held by Austria). |
| December | Prussians invade Moravia to relieve pressure on the Franco-Bavarians; the invasion falters when Austrian forces threaten Silesia. |

## 1742

| | |
|---|---|
| **24 January** | Coronation of Charles Albert von Wittelsbach as Charles VII, Holy Roman Emperor. Having driven the Franco-Bavarian forces back into Bavaria, Austrian forces under Ludwig Andreas Khevenhüller capture Munich. |
| **17 May** | Prussians defeat Austrians at Chotusitz. |
| **21 May** | First detachments of British troops land at Ostend, for service in Flanders. |
| **11 June** | Second Treaty of Breslau, signed by Austria and Prussia, brings hostilities to an end. Austria is now free to concentrate on operations in Bavaria. |
| **10 July** | Final detachment of British troops lands at Ostend, bringing the total force up to 12,076 infantry and 4,000 cavalry. |
| **July** | Britain agrees to subsidize a further 22,000 auxiliary troops drawn from Hanover and Hesse-Kassel for service in Flanders, all of which are to join the Austrian army of 14,500 men. The combined force is to be commanded by John Dalrymple, Earl of Stair. Austria rejects French peace overtures. |

## 1743

| | |
|---|---|
| **20 February** | British contingent begins to leave its cantonments in Flanders, in nine divisions, intending to cross the Rhine at Neuwied. |
| **12 March** | Allied troops cross the Rhine. |
| **27 June** | Battle of Dettingen: the French are defeated and retreat to the west bank of the Main. The Pragmatic Army crosses the Forchbach to provide cover against French troops advancing from Aschaffenburg, and encamps around the village of Hörstein. |

# OPPOSING COMMANDERS

## THE PRAGMATIC ARMY

### *George (II) Augustus, King of Great Britain, Duke of Brunswick-Lüneburg, Elector of Hanover (1683–1760)*

Despite seeing extensive service during the War of the Spanish Succession, his father's accession to the British throne in 1714 meant that George's military career was over at the age of 30. By an unhappy turn of fate, this would roughly coincide with the birth of his nephew Frederick of Prussia, who would embark upon his military career at a similar age. After the outbreak of war in 1740, a seemingly one-sided rivalry would develop, with George becoming increasingly critical and jealous of his nephew's achievements. As a result, it was a simple decision for George to delay his return from Hanover in the summer of 1743 in order to take command of the Pragmatic Army for the remainder of the campaigning season.

The problem with this was that although he had been under fire, King George had never actually commanded an army. This inexperience led him to follow the advice of civilian advisors, rather than military ones, and he was thus under no pressure to join the troops before they set out on campaign. This delay led directly to the Pragmatic Army being virtually encircled by the French forces, and the subsequent lack of direction after 19 June that led to the Pragmatic Army potentially facing an almost catastrophic defeat.

King George II of Great Britain. His desire for military glory almost compromised the Allied campaign.

### *John Dalrymple, Earl of Stair (1673–1747)*

Like many of his contemporaries, Stair would 'earn his spurs' in Flanders, firstly having served as a volunteer in the Earl of Angus' Regiment of Foot, in which unit he distinguished himself at the Battle of Steenkerke, and later under the Duke of Marlborough, under whose aegis he rose from being a captain in the 3rd Foot Guards in the early stages of the War of the Spanish Succession to being a lieutenant-general at its close.

Having acceded to the earldom upon his father's death (1707), Stair's position in court circles was assured. After the accession of King George I to the British throne in 1714, he was sent to Paris as Britain's envoy to the French court. It was a position he retained for the next six years, and during this time he became well acquainted with many of the Frenchmen he would face during the Dettingen campaign, the most notable of whom was Adrien-Maurice, Duc de Noailles.

In March 1742, Stair was appointed field marshal, and the following month he was given command of the British contingent, which would serve alongside Austrian and Hanoverian troops within the Pragmatic Army; this appointment effectively gave him the army command. During the summer of 1743, the presence of King George II with the army meant that Stair was relegated from the army command, and he tendered his resignation as soon as he felt able to do so, citing age and ill health rather than any critique of the government, which he would do in a later memorandum published towards the end of the year.

A French pistol made by the gunsmith Gilles Massin of Liège. (Reproduced with courtesy and kind permission of Musée d'Histoire Militaire, Tournai)

### Léopold Philippe Charles Joséph, Duc d'Arenberg (1690–1754)

A scion of one of Flanders' most prestigious families, Arenberg inherited his titles before his first birthday when, in August 1691, his father was killed in action at the Battle of Slankamen. Following in his father's footsteps, the young duke took service with the Austrian army in 1706, spending the remainder of the War of the Spanish Succession in Flanders, being wounded at Malplaquet in September 1709.

After the Peace of Utrecht, Arenberg found himself temporarily without military employment. However, tensions in the Balkans meant that further conflict with the Ottoman Empire was inevitable, and war was declared in 1716, with the Austrian field army being led by the talismanic Prince Eugène of Savoy. Volunteering for active service, Arenberg was appointed *General Feld Wachtmeister*, an intermediate rank roughly equivalent to the contemporary rank in the French army of *Maréchal de Camp*. Having distinguished himself during the campaign, he returned to Flanders as governor of the province of Hennegau, which was centred around Charleroi.

In 1737, he became a member of the Imperial Privy Council, and in 1742, was appointed *Feldmarschall* and military governor of the Austrian Netherlands. As the senior non-British officer serving with the Pragmatic Army, he became its de facto deputy, even in the later presence of King George II.

### Prince William Augustus, KG, KB, FRS, Duke of Cumberland (1721–65)

The sixth child, and second surviving son, of King George II, Cumberland was the first of his siblings to be born in London. As such, he was viewed by both his father and the government as a solution to a myriad of familial and political problems.

As a royal prince, William had his name placed on the rolls of the 2nd Foot Guards and was created a Knight of the Bath before his fourth birthday; before his fifth, he was invested with several titles, the principal of which being Duke of Cumberland, the title by which he is generally known.

With family tensions leading to two royal courts – that of the king and that of the Prince of Wales – Cumberland was, to a degree, groomed by his father as a possible replacement heir, should an agreeable mechanism be found that would give his elder brother the Hanoverian lands whilst he would ultimately inherit the British throne. In the end, the king's plans came to naught, and at the age of 19, the young prince elected for a career in the army.

During the early stages of the War of the Austrian Succession, Cumberland resigned his commission in order to become colonel of the 1st Foot Guards, being subsequently promoted to major-general. With the certainty that the Pragmatic Army would be engaged sometime during the summer of 1743, the duke accompanied his father on his tour of Hanover, both of them joining the army in the field shortly before the Battle of Dettingen.

# THE FRENCH

### Adrien-Maurice de Noailles, Duc de Noailles (1678–1766)

As with many of his peers, Noailles' entry into the military life came with his enlistment in the Mousquetaires du Roi in 1692, followed by a transfer into his father's cavalry regiment. A movement from the royal household troops to a regiment of the line would – in normal circumstances – have been a retrograde step, but the key to advancement was active service, and as *Noailles-père* was commanding the French army then operating in Catalonia, the Comte d'Ayen, as he was then known, spent two years serving under his father, eventually succeeding him as colonel of the regiment.

During the following decade and a half, Ayen's career was marked by both commendable service in the Low Countries, Spain and Germany, and by a steady progression through the ranks, which was only suitable for the Duc de Noailles, the title to which he had ascended upon the death of his father in 1708.

Created a Grandee of Spain in 1711, he retired from active service, and during the minority of Louis XV he became a member of the Council of State.

When the War of the Polish Succession broke out, he immediately applied for a military command, and was appointed to the Army of the Rhine (Armée du Rhin) under the Duke of Berwick, upon whose death he assumed joint command of the army, being simultaneously elevated to the marshalate. With the German theatre stabilized, Noailles transferred to Italy, where he was responsible for negotiating a favourable peace with his Austrian counterparts. But his main achievement came neither on the battlefield nor at the negotiating table; frustrated at the lethargy of French colleagues, he acted as sponsor of a German exile who had taken service with France some years previously, ultimately securing that worthy's promotion to lieutenant-general. The individual was, of course, Maurice de Saxe.

Returning to France, Noailles assumed command of all French forces in northern France and the Low Countries, his task not only being to prepare the region to repulse an enemy attack from the north, but also – as senior commander in the field – to ensure that the various French armies remained in support of each other, and thus prevented an

Adrien-Maurice, Duc de Noailles, the veteran soldier who came within an ace of defeating the Pragmatic Army at Dettingen. His protégé, Maurice de Saxe, would do so two years later at Fontenoy.

enemy thrust along army boundaries. When faced with the need to counter the march of the Pragmatic Army into Bavaria, he stripped as many troops from the border as practicable, before calling up drafts from various depots. As a result of this admixture in troop quality, he decided to implement a Fabian strategy, one that came within a whisker of success.

### Louis-Antoine, Duc de Gramont (1689–1745)

Born into one of Navarre's most prominent families, the young Comte de Lesparre – as he was then known – served initially as a gentleman-trooper in the Mousquetaires du Roi before transferring into the Gardes Françaises, which was commanded by his father, the then Duc de Gramont. Thrown almost immediately into the crucible of war, Lesparre saw action at Huy and Ramillies, after which battle (and on 30 May that year – his 17th birthday) he received the colonelcy of a regiment of dragoons. He subsequently led this unit into action at the battles of Oudenarde and Wynendaele.

Over the following years, Lesparre leapfrogged his way through commissions in increasingly more prestigious regiments, before securing a dynastic marriage with Geneviève de Gontaut, daughter of the Duc de Biron. He finally left the army in 1727.

With the outbreak of the War of the Polish Succession in 1734, Gramont petitioned for – and received – the colonelcy of the Régiment de Vermandois infantry. He was appointed *Maréchal de Camp* in the Army of the Rhine, and served at the Siege of Phillipsburg in 1734, before transferring to Italy, where he served until the cessation of hostilities.

On 1 March 1738, Gramont was one of a number of officers promoted to the rank of lieutenant-general, and on 16 May 1741, following the death of his elder brother, he acceded to the title of Duc de Gramont and the attached patrimonies, as well as becoming colonel of the Gardes Françaises, a position which had been held by both his father and his brother before him.

With the outbreak of hostilities in December 1740, Gramont was naturally at the forefront when it came to the appointment to field commands; this was in no way hindered by the fact that his maternal uncle – the Duc de Noailles – would be taking the field as the senior member of the marshalate on active service. Like a number of his contemporaries, Gramont received his appointment to the Army of the Rhine in April 1743, and would remain within its senior command throughout the campaign.

Coming into the Dettingen campaign, the main thing that can be said about Gramont's military career to date was that whilst – on paper at least – he had the experience and length of service, and had held a number of field commands, he had not served as an independent or senior commander. In short, he was a subordinate, but not a leader, and this is probably

A British pistol made by the gunsmith John Harman of London. (Reproduced with courtesy and kind permission of Musée d'Histoire Militaire, Tournai)

the principal reason that led to his being given command of the blocking force upon which Noailles' entire plan of operations was based. On one hand, whilst Gramont may have been the army commander's nephew, he also held the commensurate field rank and was commander of the king's foot guards; on the other, there was no shortage of dukes or princes within the upper echelons of Noailles' army, many of whom also had rank – both military and social – superior to Gramont's. But perhaps the key is that his service had shown no sign of a willingness to completely disregard and disobey any orders that he had been given. In fact, in the days before the battle, he had performed commendable service during the operations to contain the Allies at Aschaffenburg.

If Noailles had perhaps kept a tighter rein on his nephew, the outcome of the battle might have been different; the temptation for Gramont to act as a knight errant rather than a military commander may have been too tempting. In any event, neither Gramont nor his senior subordinates would be called to task for their actions. Gramont himself would atone by dying on the field of battle at Fontenoy in May 1745, whilst his brother-in-law – at that time the Duc de Biron – would rally the Gardes Françaises and prevent a repetition of events at Dettingen.

### Louis-Antoine de Gontaut, Duc de Biron (1701–88)

Originally destined for a career in the navy, Biron broke short his studies in order to the join the army as a *colonel réformé* in the Régiment de Chartres infantry, holding this nominal rank from 1 January 1719. Eight years later, he left the infantry to raise a company of horsemen for the Régiment de Noailles cavalry, but returned to his original arm of service upon obtaining the colonel-lieutenantcy of the Régiment Royal-Roussillon on 22 July 1729.

During the War of the Polish Succession, Biron's regiment saw considerable service in northern Italy, taking part in the storming of Pizzighettone and Milan (both 1733) and the capture of Cortona (1734), as a result of which he was appointed brigadier on 4 February of that year. Wounded at the Battle of Parma on 5 June, he then led a column on a raid that captured the Austrian general Maximilian von La Tour at the latter's field headquarters. As the campaign progressed, Biron greatly distinguished himself at the battles of La Secchia and Guastalla, his actions being such that he was entrusted with a number of independent commands, all of which he executed with success.

After the end of the war (like many of his peers), he returned to France, where, on 29 February 1740, he became Duc de Biron (his eldest surviving brother having decided to join the Church). Appointed to the Army of Bohemia, he took part in the capture of Prague, and then served in Moravia, until resurgent Austrian forces drove the French back into the Bohemian capital. During the summer of 1742, with Prague besieged by Austrian forces under Georg von Lobkowitz, Biron led two sorties in as many days. During the first, his troops stormed one of the principal enemy batteries, spiking the guns, destroying a considerable section of siege-works and capturing

Reconstruction of the uniform of the Chevau-légers de la Garde du Roy. (Copyright and reproduced with kind permission of Gabriele Mendella)

Reconstruction of the uniform of a French infantryman of the Royal-Rousillon. (Copyright and reproduced with kind permission of Gabriele Mendella)

Lobkowitz's chief of engineers. During the second, he again attacked the enemy works, but as he encouraged his men to drag away some Austrian cannon as prizes, he was hit twice by enemy fire – the first musket ball hitting him in the jaw, whilst the second fractured his skull and had to be removed by an emergency trepanning procedure.

Despite the seriousness of his wounds, Biron survived the army's retreat back to France, where he was appointed lieutenant-general, his new rank dating from 20 February 1743. As a veteran and proven officer, his services were much in demand, and – for reasons other than those for his brother-in-law, the Duc de Gramont – it was perhaps also inevitable that Biron would find himself under the command of the Duc de Noailles.

### François, Duc d'Harcourt (1689–1750)

The young Marquis d'Harcourt took his first steps on the military ladder when, at the age of 16, he raised a regiment of cavalry for royal service. However, like Gramont, he soon eschewed this original command for a position in the Mousquetaires, considering it more fitting for the son and heir of one of France's premier dukes. Again, like Gramont, Harcourt saw service in Flanders during Marlborough's campaigns, and fought at Ramillies and Oudenarde. In July 1709, he transferred to the Army of the Rhine, which was commanded by his father. He discharged his duties competently, and was able – on 9 April 1712 – to assume command of the Régiment du Dauphin cavalry. The following year, he participated in the capture of several important German towns and cities, such as Speyer, Worms, Kaiserslautern and Freiburg.

In 1715, Harcourt left his regiment to join the 3e Compagnie des Gardes du Corps, one of his father's military sinecures, rising to command the unit upon the death of his father in 1718 and his own accession to the ducal title. Appointed *Maréchal de Camp* in April 1727, he was transferred to the Army of Italy upon the outbreak of the War of the Polish Succession. There, his career mirrored that of Biron, being promoted to lieutenant-general on 1 August 1734, and at Guastalla he led the French cavalry to victory over their Austrian counterparts, being lightly wounded in the process.

The following year, Harcourt spent much of his time in the reduction of enemy strongpoints. As the war declined in intensity, he returned to France, where he was given the governorship of Sédan in lieu of the Maréchal de Coigny, who had assumed similar duties in Alsace. In February 1742, Harcourt was appointed to the Army of Bavaria, where his command was deployed in what is now the state of Baden-Württemburg. He consolidated the French position to such a degree that the Austrian forces made no attempt to dislodge his troops from their positions, preferring to engage easier targets instead.

In April 1743, Harcourt was appointed to the Army of the Rhine, and on 27 June, he commanded the French right wing at the Battle of Dettingen, where he received a number of wounds riding in the front rank of the Maison du Roi.

# OPPOSING FORCES

Traditionally, the Battle of Dettingen is viewed as being a combat fought between Britain and France, an assertion that is understandable, but incorrect. In the summer of 1743, neither of the two nations was actually at war with the other; instead, they were serving as auxiliaries of other powers. The battle was actually fought between the forces of His Imperial Majesty Charles VII, Holy Roman Emperor and Electoral Prince of Bavaria (the French) and those of Her Royal Majesty Maria Theresia, Queen of Hungary and Archduchess of Austria et al. (the British and Hanoverian elements of the Pragmatic Army).

In terms of numbers, the two forces were very unequal, with Noailles' French army numbering something in the region of 70,000 effectives, whilst the Earl of Stair (and then King George II) fielded just over 45,000 men. The number of troops in either army is misleading in itself: Noailles' battle plan involved engaging the enemy from a number of different directions almost simultaneously (thus contravening the military adage of never dividing your forces whilst in proximity to the enemy), whereas the Pragmatic Army would fight as a single unit. In effect, the battle would be fought by approximately 30,000 Frenchmen under the Duc de Gramont and 45,000 Allied troops under King George, the numerical advantage lying firmly with the Allies.

At the tactical level, there were naturally several differences between the armies. Although French regiments could contain one or several subunits, she had long sought to standardize her brigade-size formations by limiting them to between four and five elements of whatever arm of service. There were naturally exceptions to this, such as the Maison du Roi or the Carabiniers, but in the main it meant that the unwieldiness of earlier armies was mitigated. Within the Pragmatic Army, there was no such standardization; Anglo-Hanoverian infantry regiments were generally single battalions, whilst Austrian units could consist of up to three battalions, with cavalry regiments of all nationalities generally containing between two and four squadrons.

Whilst cavalry formations generally formed on similar lines, there were naturally differences in formation and doctrine between the two armies. The Austrians and Hanoverians on one side and the French on the other both favoured deeper formations, whilst the British – using the writings of General Humphrey Bland – were beginning to emphasize firepower rather than close combat, and were tending towards shallower formations that would allow more muskets to bear upon the enemy. In terms of the latter,

# The political situation, early 1743

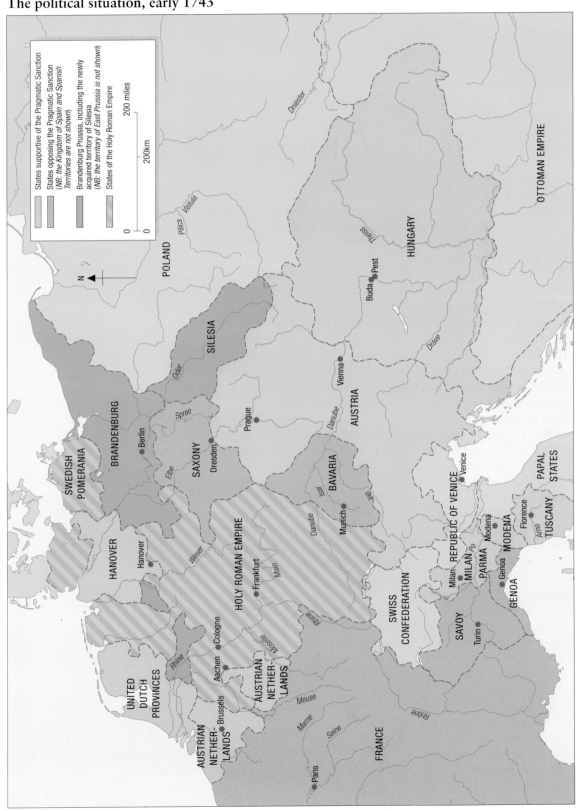

Legend:
- States supportive of the Pragmatic Sanction
- States opposing the Pragmatic Sanction (*NB: the Kingdom of Spain and Spanish Territories are not shown*)
- Brandenburg Prussia, including the newly acquired territory of Silesia (*NB: the territory of East Prussia is not shown*)
- States of the Holy Roman Empire

200 miles
200km

OTTOMAN EMPIRE

POLAND

HUNGARY
Buda Pest

Thiess

Drave

SILESIA

Oder

BRANDENBURG
Berlin

Spree

SAXONY
Dresden

Prague

AUSTRIA
Vienna

Danube

SWEDISH POMERANIA

Elbe

BAVARIA
Isar
Munich

Inn

REPUBLIC OF VENICE
Venice

PAPAL STATES

HANOVER
Hanover

Weser

Danube

HOLY ROMAN EMPIRE
Frankfurt

Main

SWISS CONFEDERATION

MILAN
Milan
PARMA
MODENA
Modena
Genoa
GENOA
Po

TUSCANY
Florence
Arno

Rhine

Moselle

Cologne
Aachen

AUSTRIAN NETHER- LANDS

Rhine

UNITED DUTCH PROVINCES

AUSTRIAN NETHER- LANDS
Brussels

Meuse

SAVOY
Turin

Marne

Seine

Rhone

FRANCE

Paris

and similar to the question of armour, speed and firepower that would plague naval theoreticians of the late 19th century, there were two theories as to infantry firepower. The French favoured a .69-calibre bullet with the view that a lighter bullet would require a smaller powder charge and thus reduce the chances of the musket fouling; whilst the British preferred a .75-calibre, which being heavier, had more 'stopping power'. Austrian and Hanoverian firearms would have tended towards the larger calibre, both in terms of self-produced weapons and those supplied by Great Britain.

With regard to artillery, the Allies had – in theory at least – an overwhelming superiority in firepower, with an estimated 80–90 cannon compared to 16 for the French. The inherent problem here was not only that the guns were almost exclusively three-pounders, and thus only effective

Highland Infantry, 1743 – a print by Richard Knötel.

at short ranges, but also (naturally enough) that, in order to be brought into action, they had to be drawn across fields full of unharvested crops, which caused delays and exhausted the crews and draught animals. Where the French had a decided, and almost battle-winning, superiority was in the 40 12lb cannons that Noailles had deployed around Mainflingen,

in order to enfilade the advancing enemy columns. Had Gramont obeyed his orders, it is not inconceivable that the French heavy batteries would have either caused such prohibitive damage in the enemy ranks so as to render an assault across the Forchbach almost impossible, or have damaged them sufficiently for Tingry's command (when it came up) to seal a French victory – one that, like Fontenoy two years later, had the potential to change the course of the war.

**FAR LEFT**
Reconstruction of the uniform of a private soldier in the Royal North British Fusiliers (21st Foot). (Copyright and reproduced with kind permission of Gabriele Mendella)

**LEFT**
Reconstruction of the uniform of the 2e Compagnie des Mousquetaires du Roi. (Copyright and reproduced with kind permission of Gabriele Mendella)

# ORDERS OF BATTLE

## THE PRAGMATIC ARMY, 27 JUNE 1743[1]

Commander: His Majesty George II Augustus, King of England, Elector of Hanover

### LEFT WING

Commander: William Augustus, Duke of Cumberland;[2] General Sir Philip Honywood

**1st Line (Lieutenant-General John Campbell of Mamore; Lieutenant-General Sir John Cope)**
King's Own Royal Regiment of Dragoons – Bland's (three squadrons)
Duke of Somerset's Regiment of Horse[3] (three squadrons)
His Majesty's Life Guards[4] (three squadrons)
Earl of Stair's Regiment of Dragoons (three squadrons)
Royal Regiment of Dragoons – Hawley's (three squadrons)

**2nd Line (Lieutenant-General Henry Hawley; Lieutenant-General John Ligonier)**
Ligonier's Regiment of Horse (two squadrons)
Honywood's Regiment of Horse (three squadrons)
Rich's Regiment of Dragoons (three squadrons)
Queen's Own Royal Regiment of Dragoons – Cope's (three squadrons)

**3rd Line (Generalmajor Louis Auguste du Verger de Monroy – Hanover)**
Monroy Regiment of Foot (Hanover)
Zastrow Regiment of Foot (Hanover)
Böselager Regiment of Foot (Hanover)
Middachten Regiment of Foot (Hanover)
Sommerfeld Regiment of Foot (Hanover)

**4th Line (General Jacques d'Amproux de Pontpietin; General Adolf Ludwig von Diemar; Generalmajor Johann Carl von Montigny; Feldmarschallleutnant de Courrières)**
Bremer Cuirassiers (Hanover) (two squadrons)
Schultzen Cuirassiers (Hanover) (two squadrons)
Lüneburg-Styrum Dragoons (Austria) (five squadrons)
De Ligne Dragoons (Austria) (five squadrons)

**5th Line (Generalmajor Christian Ludwig von Hammerstein-Loxten)**
Leibregiment zu Pferd (Hanover) (two squadrons)
Wrede Cuirassiers (Hanover) (two squadrons)
Hammerstein Cuirassiers (Hanover) (two squadrons)

**6th Line (Generalmajor Georg von Launay)**
Garde Grenadiere zu Pferd (Hanover)
Gardes du Corps (Hanover)
Montigny Cuirassiers (Hanover) (two squadrons)
Bülow Cuirassiers (Hanover) (two squadrons)

### CENTRE

Commander: Feldmarschall Duke of Arenberg; Feldmarschall Georg Wilhelm, Prince von Hessen-Darmstadt

**1st Line (Feldmarschall Wilhelm Reinhard, Graf von Neipperg; Lieutenant-General Ludwig Ernst, Prince von Braunschweig-Wolfenbüttel)**
De Ligne Regiment of Foot (Austrian)
Los Rios Regiment of Foot (Austrian) (two battalions)
Prié Regiment of Foot (Austrian)

Wolfenbüttel Regiment of Foot[5] (Austrian)

**2nd Line (Lieutenant-General Karl Urban, Graf von Chanclos)**
Arenberg Regiment of Foot (Austrian) (two battalions)
Gaisrück Regiment of Foot (Austrian) (two battalions)
Wolfenbüttel Regiment of Foot (Austrian)

**3rd Line (Lieutenant-General Jasper Clayton)**
Thomas Howard's Regiment of Foot
Johnson's Regiment of Foot
Earl of Rothes' Regiment of Foot
Duroure's Regiment of Foot
Onslow's Regiment of Foot
Pulteney's Regiment of Foot

**4th Line (Lieutenant-General Nikolaus Leopold, Graf von Salm)**
Arenberg Regiment of Foot (Austrian) (two battalions)
Salm Regiment of Foot (Austrian)
Heister Regiment of Foot (Austrian)
Royal Regiment of Welsh Fuziliers
Ponsonby's Regiment of Foot

### RIGHT WING

Commander: Field Marshal John Dalrymple, 2nd Earl of Stair

**1st Line**
Handasyde's Regiment of Foot
Charles Howard's Regiment of Foot
Huske's Regiment of Foot
Royal North British Fusiliers

**2nd Line**
Wrangel's Regiment of Foot (Hanover)
Soubiron's Regiment of Foot (Hanover)
Borch's Regiment of Foot (Hanover)
Schulenberg's Regiment of Foot (Hanover)

**3rd Line (General Franz Karl von Wendt)**
Pontpietin Dragoons (Hanover) (four squadrons)
Bussche Dragoons (Hanover) (four squadrons)
Adlepsen Dragoons (Hanover) (four squadrons)
Wendt Dragoons (Hanover) (four squadrons)

**Rear-guard[6] (Lieutenant-General Thomas von Ilten)**
Campe Regiment of Foot (Hanover)
Jung-Spörken Regiment of Foot (Hanover)
Garde zu Fuss (Hanover) (two battalions)
His Majesty's Foot Guards[7] (three battalions)
Royal North British Dragoons (three squadrons)

## THE FRENCH ARMY AT DETTINGEN, JUNE 1743

Commander: Adrien Maurice de Noailles, Duc de Noailles, Maréchal de France

### DETTINGEN

Commander: Duc de Gramont
**Maison du Roi (Gardes Bleus)**
Grenadiers à Cheval
1er Compagnie, Garde du Corps (Écossaise) (two squadrons)
2e Compagnie, Garde du Corps (Française) (two squadrons)
3e Compagnie, Garde du Corps (Française) (two squadrons)
4e Compagnie, Garde du Corps (Française) (two squadrons)
**Maison du Roi (Gardes Rouges)**
Mousquetaires du Roi (two squadrons)

---

1  Units are listed as they deployed, in order from left to right in the line of battle. Where no nationality is given in brackets, the unit concerned is British. The number of battalions or squadrons is given in brackets; where there is no number, it is a single formation.
2  Where an officer had several titles, only the principal one by which they are known is given here.
3  From 1750, 'The Royal Horse Guards'.
4  3rd and 4th troops of Life Guards, 2nd Troop of Life Grenadier Guards.

5  This was a two-battalion regiment of Austrian Foot with one battalion in each of the 2nd and 3rd lines.
6  Eventually moved up to deploy behind the 3rd Line of the Right Wing.
7  1st Regiment of Foot Guards, Coldstream Regiment of Foot Guards, 3rd Regiment of Foot Guards.

Chevau-légers de la Garde
Gendarmes de la Garde
**Brigade des Cuirassiers**
Royal Cuirassiers (three squadrons)
Andlau
Gramont (two squadrons)
**Brigade des Carabiniers**
Carabiniers (five reinforced squadrons)
Penthièvre (two squadrons)
Chabot (two squadrons)
**Brigade de France-Royal**
France-Royal (two squadrons)
Fleury
Noailles (two squadrons)
**Brigade de Dragons**
Bauffremont (four squadrons)
Mailly (four squadrons)
Mestre de Camp (five squadrons)
**Brigade Berchény**
Berchény Hussars
Esterházy Hussars
**Gardes Françaises**
Gardes Françaises (six battalions)
**Brigade Orléans**
Orléans (two battalions)
Royal La Marine
Vexin
**Brigade Touraine**
Touraine (three battalions)
Chartres (two battalions)
**Brigade Auvergne**
Auvergne (two battalions)
Condé (two battalions)
Artois
**Brigade Noailles**
Noailles (three battalions)
Hainault
La Marche
**Brigade Piémont**
Piémont (four battalions)
Nice
**Brigade Rohan**
Rohan (three battalions)
Dauphiné
Aubeterre
**Brigade d'Eu**
Eu (two battalions)
Penthièvre (two battalions)
Mortemart
**Brigade du Roi**
Le Roi (four battalions)
Biron

**Brigade Navarre**
Navarre (four battalions)
Bigorre

## STOCKSTADT

Commander: Duc de Noailles
**Brigade Mestre de Camp**
Mestre de Camp (two squadrons)
Chabrillant (two squadrons)
Prince de Clermont (three squadrons)
**Brigade Egmont**
Egmont (two squadrons)
Vintimille (two squadrons)
Royal Cravattes (three squadrons)
**Brigade Royal-Pologne**
Royal-Pologne (three squadrons)
Vogué (two squadrons)
Talleyrand (two squadrons)
**Brigade Colonel-Général**
Colonel-Général (two squadrons)
La Reine (two squadrons)
Clermont-Tonnerre (two squadrons)
**Brigade Brancas**
Brancas (three squadrons)
Le Roi (two squadrons)

## ASCHAFFENBURG

Commander: Prince de Tingry
**Brigade de la Marine**
La Marine (four battalions)
Nivernais
**Brigade Brancas**
Brancas (two battalions)
Gardes Lorraines
Forez
**Brigade Dauphin**
Dauphin (two battalions)
Béarn
Bassigny
Beaujolais
**Brigade Irlandaise**
Berwick
Rooth
Dillon
Clare
Bulkeley

## MAINFLINGEN

Commander: Jean Florent de la Vallière
40 12lb cannon

# OPPOSING PLANS

## THE PRAGMATIC ARMY

If the definition of a battle plan is the choice of an objective coupled with a series of tactical manoeuvres intended to create the circumstances with which to achieve that objective, then the unfortunate truth is that – at Dettingen – there was no Allied plan of battle.

As a result of the council of war, all that the Allies had was an objective: the magazine at Hanau. There, they intended to resupply and await reinforcement, but until news came that the French had crossed the Main and were now deployed across their line of march, they had had no inclination that a battle was imminent. From this point on, the Pragmatic Army was forced almost entirely into a reactive posture.

In the face of the enemy action, and once Generalfeldwachtmeister Count O'Donnel's report had worked its way up the chain of command, the only viable series of orders open to the Allies was to halt the march and try to reorganize the army in such a fashion as to provide some semblance of a line of battle. This meant that instead of fighting together, the troops of the three contingents would now be spread across the battlefield as either chance (with the British deploying in the centre and the right flank, the Austrians in the centre and the left flank and the Hanoverians on either flank), or terrain (with almost all of the Allied cavalry deploying on the left wing) dictated.

This would naturally lead to confusion, not only in the relaying of orders or where senior officers stood in the hierarchy of these ad hoc commands, but crucially it led to the placing of Monroy's Hanoverian infantry brigade directly in the middle of Cumberland's almost exclusively cavalry wing. It was an unfortunate trick of fate, which meant that less than half of the Allied cavalry would be able to be employed, until such time as the terrain had sufficiently opened

Lock detail of a British Land Pattern Tower Musket 'Brown Bess'. (Reproduced with courtesy and kind permission of Musée d'Histoire Militaire, Tournai)

# The strategic situation, May–June 1743

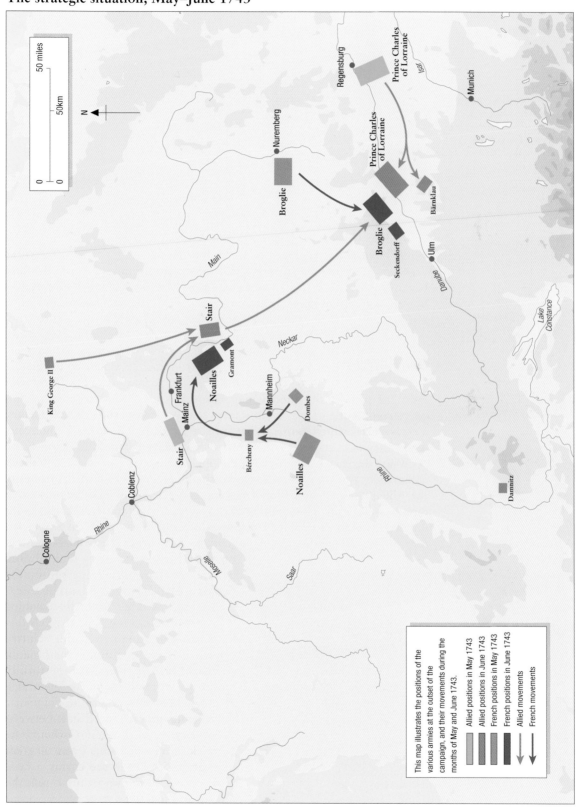

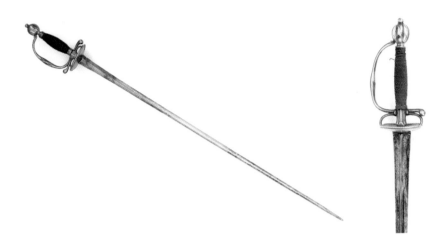

up to allow the remaining horsemen to skirt the Hanoverian infantrymen. It would have almost fatal consequences for the Allies.

Once the Pragmatic Army had settled into an offensive posture and begun its advance, any plans that may now have been mooted were almost immediately cast aside when Gramont inexplicably abandoned his defensive position and crossed to the south of the Forchbach stream.

## THE FRENCH

From the outset of the campaigning season, Noailles had been determined to only accept battle under circumstances that he deemed to be advantageous, a stance exemplified by his refusal to rise to the bait and attack the Allies whilst they were strongly entrenched at Höchst, near Frankfurt.

When the enemy withdrew to the opposite side of the Main, the French commander was more than happy to shadow them, certain that eventually the Allied commanders would make a mistake. There were at least three months before the campaigning season would come to an end, and other opportunities for a decisive battle would undoubtedly arise. In any event, for as long as the Pragmatic Army remained in Hesse, it was unable to link up with the Austrian army under Prince Charles of Lorraine. As a result, the position of the Franco-Bavarian forces in Bavaria, his other concern, remained eminently stable.

When the enemy left the relative safety of Hanau, continuing their march southwards, Noailles was naturally more than content to follow them at a distance. However, when the Pragmatic Army made its prolonged halt between Aschaffenburg and Klein-Ostheim, he knew that he had been given a great opportunity to strike the enemy a fatal blow. It was an opportunity that he intended to make the most of.

The Main footbridge near Mainflingen. During the summer of 1743, the entire foreground would have been under several feet of water.

## Noailles' plan of operations

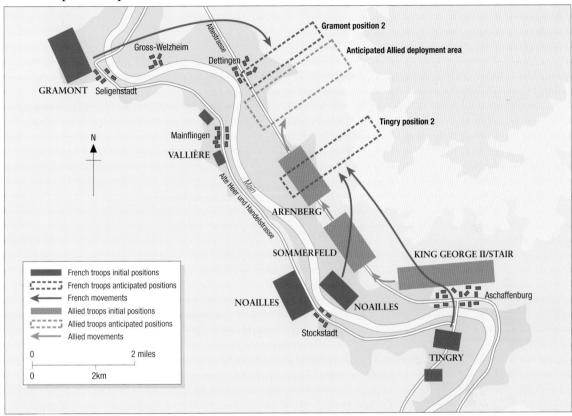

French troops initial positions
French troops anticipated positions
French movements
Allied troops initial positions
Allied troops anticipated positions
Allied movements

0       2 miles
0       2km

It should be stressed that Noailles' sole priority was the defeat of the Pragmatic Army, and the later presence of King George II with the army was incidental to his planning. As far as the Frenchman was concerned, the initiative lay in his hands, and there was no need for rash or precipitate action: he could afford to wait and consider his options, allowing the odds to stack up in his favour.

The first step was to establish control of the Main both above and below the enemy position, a measure which was completed relatively easily by the deployment of several blocking forces supported by artillery. With the river cut, the Allies' sole logistical artery was the Alte Heer und Handelstrasse, based upon the roadways used in antiquity to move troops and supplies along Rome's border with the unconquered Germanic tribes. As a communications link, the road was excellent, but its use was limited by the fact that in order to avoid the flood plain, the road crossed the Main at Gross-Welzheim/ Seligenstadt, so as to take advantage of the higher ground on the river's western bank. The road that continued south towards Aschaffenburg, and the one which the Allies would need to use, was in comparison little more than a dirt track.

Hilt detail of a French cavalryman's sword. (Reproduced with courtesy and kind permission of Musée d'Histoire Militaire, Tournai)

French 12lb cannon of the Vallière system. The gun has a calibre of 121mm and a barrel length of 2.9m. The shape of the cascabel denotes the weight of shot. (PHGCOM via Wikimedia Commons, CC BY-SA 3.0)

As soon as the French troops had arrived in the vicinity of the Allied encampments, the first task to be undertaken was the establishment of a strong bridgehead on the enemy bank opposite Stockstadt, followed by the detachment of a blocking force to cover the southern entrance to the stone bridge at Aschaffenburg. In these two movements, the beginnings of Noailles' plan can be seen.

It should be noted that the Main River in 1743 was far wider and shallower, albeit with a higher water level; the current course is dictated by the dredging and straightening of the river during the modern industrial era. In effect, this meant that the Main could only be crossed at bridges or fords. This naturally meant that unless either of the opposing commanders were prepared to hazard a river crossing under fire, it would act as a cordon sanitaire between the two armies. This situation was made more complicated by the fact that to the east of the Allies lay the Spessart Hills, an area of wooded high ground that was a natural obstacle to the movement of large bodies of troops or wheeled transport.

In short, whilst the French enjoyed full freedom of movement, the Allies were deployed in a very narrow corridor, their only options being to move forward or backward.

Correctly anticipating that the Allies' failure to secure the crossing at Aschaffenburg would now oblige them to retrace their steps to the magazine at Hanau, Noailles began to put the final parts of his plan in place: the Irish Brigade was to move up to Aschaffenburg, whilst Berchény's hussars were to rejoin the main body of the army. When the Irishmen reached their destination, the blocking force would total some 14 battalions of foot, a sufficient number of men to defeat any attempt by the enemy to force a crossing under fire.

For Noailles, this was just a security measure. Trusting in his earlier judgement that the enemy would withdraw towards Hanau, he moved three brigades of infantry, two of heavy cavalry and one of dragoons, together with two batteries of artillery and the Maison du Roi, to Seligenstadt. His intention was to throw this force across the Main and place it athwart the Hanau road. Whichever way the Allies chose to move, they would find their passage blocked and their rear threatened by significant bodies of French troops, the remainder of Noailles' command being held at Stockstadt to reinforce either body or to drive straight across the Main as circumstances dictated.

To complete the trap, a total of 40 12lb cannon – deployed in five batteries – were to be sited on the higher west bank of the Main near Mainflingen, their placement being personally overseen by Jean Florent de la Vallière, the King's Inspector-General of Artillery. With the enemy unable to either advance or retreat, and with their flanks blocked by natural obstacles, these heavy guns, initially firing from concealed positions, would be the key to Noailles' plan. Their task was to rake the enemy lines with plunging enfilade fire until the time came to deliver the *coup de grâce*.

# THE CAMPAIGN

## BAITING THE TRAP

The catalyst for the 1743 Main campaign came about not through the actions of the principal combatants, but rather through the political dexterity that brought about a diplomatic settlement between Austria and Prussia over the contested province of Silesia. The signing of the Second Treaty of Breslau (11 June 1742) permitted Prussia to consolidate her hold on the region, whilst Austrian forces were allowed to withdraw unmolested from the theatre of operations for redeployment elsewhere. As such, it was inevitable that they would be committed against the Franco-Bavarian forces in Bavaria, which now – having already lost the capital, Munich – stood firmly on the defensive.

With her armies stretched in a line running eastwards from the Channel coast into the Rhine Valley and the German states, the arrival of these fresh enemy troops stretched the French forces to almost breaking point. The decisions that would soon be made at Versailles would naturally dictate the

These contemporary maps (hand-painted upon leather panels) show the area between Hanau and the battlefield of Dettingen.

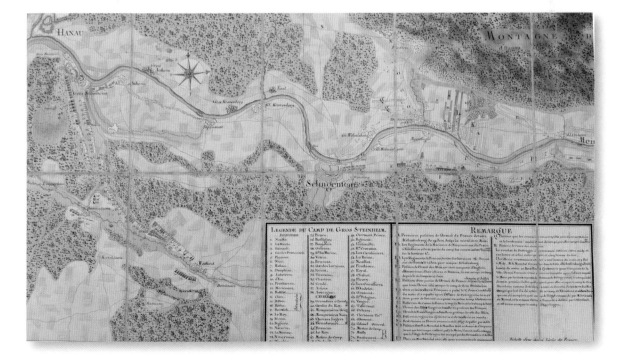

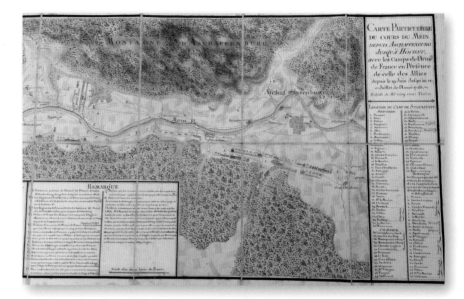

A panel from the same map, showing the area between the battlefield of Dettingen and Aschaffenburg.

course of the war as a whole. Politically, France was committed to defend Bavaria, both as a long-standing ally and also as a counterweight to the Austrian Hapsburgs; this meant that she needed to counter the arrival of fresh Austrian troops and urgently reinforce the Franco-Bavarian forces under the joint command of Friedrich von Seckendorff and the Duc de Broglie.

In theory, the necessity was an easy one to identify, but a difficult one to resolve. French military thinking was still based – to a large degree – upon Vaubanesque principles. In short, it was a system of checks and balances, whereby the need to protect potential targets under one's own control was balanced against establishing a threat or threats against targets in enemy territory, in order to dissuade the enemy from taking offensive action.

Unfortunately for France, the only available formation large enough and close enough in position to effectively intervene in Bavaria was the Army of Westphalia (Armée de Westphalie), commanded by the Marquis de Maillebois. The problem was that Maillebois' principal tasks were to cover the Rhine and threaten the Electorate of Hanover, thus polarizing the attention of the British crown. The question facing Versailles was therefore whether to redeploy Maillebois' command, or instead to trust that Broglie and Seckendorff could – between them – reverse the current trend, regaining both the initiative and the lost territory in Bavaria.

Eventually, the marquis was indeed ordered to move his command south-eastwards in support of the Franco-Bavarian forces. Whilst this naturally uncovered Hanover and removed any direct French threat to the electorate, it should be noted that it also placed an additional line of troops to protect France's western flank against an Austrian thrust from Bavaria. Strategically, this shift in French policy now led to two fundamental changes in the situation on the frontier. Firstly, the various French armies would now come under the oversight of the Duc de Noailles, whose task was to cover Germany whilst also protecting French interests. Secondly, the Allies were no longer obliged to wait for an inevitable French attack; they were, instead, able to take the field themselves.

With responsibility for the entire frontier, Noailles – initially working from an office at the Palace of Versailles – was faced with an almost herculean task. Given the breadth of his remit, the initiative lay naturally with the Allies, who could mass to attack at a single point, whilst Noailles had to arrange sufficient cover for the whole area under his responsibility.

Therefore, in December 1742, the marshal sent several commissary officers out into the field; their task was to report upon the combat readiness of all garrisons and military posts, and make recommendations to resolve any deficiencies that they might find. Additionally, he sent a Flemish nobleman, the Comte de Bergeyck, into the Austrian Netherlands to observe and report upon the strength and dispositions of the enemy forces there. Bergeyck, whose family had long served in the government of the former Spanish Netherlands, was the perfect choice to gather this vital intelligence, as his family pedigree granted him access and immunities that others simply lacked.

Having set these measures in train, Noailles now had to consider how best to deploy the remainder of his forces. In effect, his options came down to one of two choices. He could either establish a series of mutually supporting *corps d'observation*, or alternately mass the bulk of his troops in one or possibly two bodies in the hope that he had divined the enemy's campaign objectives correctly.

Front cover of the French periodical *Le Miroir du Monde* from 1930, showing the recreation of the Battle of Dettingen at the Aldershot Military Tattoo.

Each option had both positive and negative aspects. If he chose to deploy his forces in several bodies, they would naturally be able to protect the greatest possible area, but the implicit risk was that the enemy could strike a single point with overwhelming numbers and secure a significant victory whilst French reinforcements were still marching to the battlefield. On the other hand, if Noailles kept his main body largely concentrated, but failed to correctly judge the enemy's plan of campaign, he could easily find his army in the wrong place at the wrong time, thereby gifting the tactical and strategic advantage to the enemy.

In the end, the decision was taken from the Frenchman's hands when Bergeyck returned to the duke's headquarters and informed him that in mid-December, a significant number of Austrian troops had left their winter quarters in Flanders and were heading towards the Duchy of Luxembourg, followed closely by the Anglo-Hanoverian contingent of the Pragmatic Army.

Naturally enough, this unexpected redeployment failed to provide Noailles with any definite clues as to the enemy's campaign objective. All it did was suggest that whatever the Allies' intentions were, they intended to remain passive in the Low Countries. The reverse of this particular coin was that the Frenchman could not afford to ignore the movement, and was therefore forced to follow in the enemy's wake until their designs became clearer. In effect, this meant that the French were also forced to forgo any offensive operations in Flanders. On the one hand, this would permit Noailles to reduce certain garrisons in order to increase the size of his field army, but it would also mean that, for the time being at least, the initiative would remain firmly with the Allies, and he would need to follow them wherever they led him. The only question remaining to be answered was whether the enemy intended to fight on the Upper Rhine, on the Moselle or somewhere further east.

A British print showing the Battle of Dettingen, as viewed from Aschaffenburg. Seligenstadt is shown in roughly the actual position of Stockstadt.

As January 1743 turned to February, the Allies remained in their new cantonments. For his part, Noailles bombarded his superiors with seemingly endless memoranda as to the potential enemy plans, submitting suggestions for the strengthening of the frontiers for which he was responsible, and even going so far as to request that drafts of replacements intended to bolster the French forces in Bavaria (which was, after all, the primary theatre of operations) be diverted instead to Lower Alsace, which he felt was under threat of a sudden enemy advance. Amongst these ideas and requests was one that would have an important influence on that summer's campaign: the creation of a park of heavy artillery, to be initially based upon the fortress of Metz.

Mid-month, the Allies finally made their move, with the British infantry leapfrogging their Austrian allies and marching further east to reach the Rhine near Düsseldorf, before turning southwards, with the Hanoverians following a similar course.[8] As the southernmost of the Allied contingents, the Austrians advanced directly into the Palatinate, heading in the direction of Trier, before pushing on to the town of Andernach, which they reached on 3 April. There, they were joined by the remainder of the army over the course of the following two weeks. Whatever the Allied plans may have been at this point in time, they were rendered moot by the news of the death of the Prince-Archbishop of Mainz on 21 March.

The importance of the elector's death was that, during the previous imperial election, he had been one of the three men who had actively supported the candidacy of the Hapsburg nominee. If Vienna were to have any say in the future administration of the Holy Roman Empire, she needed to ensure that Mainz was ruled by someone at best well disposed or at worst neutral to her. If a pro-Bavarian candidate were to assume power in the electorate,

---

8   The Anglo-Hanoverian cavalry would remain in the Low Countries until the weather conditions improved and facilitated their movement. They would then move via Aachen, and would catch up with the main body of the army in early May.

she would have an unassailable majority in the Imperial College, and this would spell the end of the Hapsburg ambitions. Mainz, therefore, needed to be preserved, and to that end, the Pragmatic Army changed its direction of march and headed south-east towards the troubled archbishopric.

Aware of the political pitfalls that lay ahead, Noailles sought guidance from his political masters, asking for clarification as to how he should deal not only with the new elector (assuming an election had already been held), but also with the numerous Germanic princelings he would encounter in the execution of his duties. In due course, a courier arrived from Versailles carrying a dispatch bearing the royal seal: the king had seen fit to appoint Noailles commander-in-chief of all French troops in Germany. His principal rules of engagement were to:

> attack the enemy wheresoever and whenever you deem the conditions most favourable, to engage them on whichever side of the Rhine they may be found and in whichever lands or territories they may be found – whether within the Empire or the Lands of the House of Austria – the sole exception to this being the Duchy of Luxembourg and the other provinces of the Low Countries, where the king forbids him to commit hostilities in his name.

Delivered in such terms, and the caveat regarding the Austrian Netherlands notwithstanding, the orders were totally unequivocal. Noailles was to pursue the Pragmatic Army wherever it went, bring it to battle on favourable terms and destroy it. Indeed, one of the final clauses within the commission went so far as to state that if the campaign were to require joint or concerted action between the French armies in Germany and Bavaria, Noailles would have the sole authority over both forces. There would be no 'command by committee', and any tactical or strategic decisions were to be his and his alone.

Gradually, the French forces destined for service in the field also left their winter quarters. The militia was called into being, and troops were drawn from Flanders (now widely regarded as a secondary theatre) that would be used to replace those troops in the Messin (the territory around the fortress-city of Metz) who were destined for active service in the field. Towards the end of February, the troops of the Maison du Roi left Paris, whilst on 21 March, the core of Noailles' army began to assemble in the Palatinate near Speyer, under the command of the Prince de Dombes, one of Louis XIV's grandsons. By the end of March, there were some 14 battalions and 44 squadrons under arms, with a further 12 battalions and 14 squadrons at Heidelberg. As further detachments and senior officers arrived, the French strength grew daily, bringing them parity and then numerical superiority over the Pragmatic Army. However, even as he was preparing for his own campaign, Noailles was to receive almost catastrophic news from Bavaria.

Having found that the Franco-Bavarian forces opposing him were effectively operating as two separate armies, Prince Charles of Lorraine had simply fallen first upon the French and then upon the Bavarians, driving a wedge between them. The situation in the south now rested firmly on a knife-edge, as the twin defeats could easily either presage an invasion of the Palatinate from Upper Bavaria, or they could signal the passing of the Pragmatic Army into Bavaria to complete the conquest of the electorate once and for all.

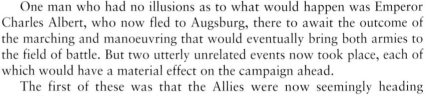

This (presumably) French watercolour map shows not only the Battle of Dettingen, but also the French positions beforehand. Note the corrected misspelling of Aschaffenburg.

One man who had no illusions as to what would happen was Emperor Charles Albert, who now fled to Augsburg, there to await the outcome of the marching and manoeuvring that would eventually bring both armies to the field of battle. But two utterly unrelated events now took place, each of which would have a material effect on the campaign ahead.

The first of these was that the Allies were now seemingly heading towards the city of Frankfurt (am Main) in the Landgraviate of Hesse-Cassel. If Noailles were to follow his orders to the letter, he would need to secure permission to enter Hessian territory. It was a requirement that would tax Noailles' diplomatic ability, not least because the Landgraf Frederick was also King of Sweden, but because Frederick's younger brother Wilhelm was head of the regency government that handled Cassel's daily affairs – and Wilhelm had a negative view of French interference in German matters. In the end, it would be diplomatic finesse that would be required, rather than the usual tactics employed by French forces operating east of the Rhine.

The second development was the arrival of His Britannic Majesty King George II on his regular summer visit to the Electorate of Hanover. There were tensions between the king and his more warlike nephew, Frederick of Prussia, and it had been suggested that with both British and Hanoverian troops forming part of the Pragmatic Army, if the king were to join them in the field, it would serve to raise both his domestic profile and the standing of the House of Hanover in especial; additionally, it would give warning to any critics there might be amongst the crowned heads of Europe. As a result, a regular courier service was established between the army's headquarters and wherever the royal suite was staying, as a precursor to the king joining the army once his personal business in Hanover was completed. It was to be a decision that would have potentially disastrous consequences for the army.

Reconstruction of the uniform of the 3e Compagnie des Gardes du Corps. (Copyright and reproduced with kind permission of Gabriele Mendella)

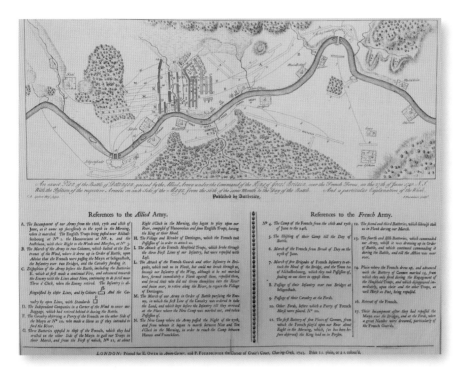

Plan of the Battle of Dettingen, London, 1743. In this clearly annotated overview, the final encampment is shown as being between Dettingen and Hörstein, rather than on the battlefield itself as quoted by many sources.

With the course of the Main River now dividing the French and Allied forces, Marshal Noailles was given an almost unprecedented latitude both in the development and execution of his plan. Until the time came to spring the trap, all movements would be made out of sight of the enemy, whilst (where possible) his own piquets and patrols would be pushing up almost to the outer reaches of the enemy encampment itself.

On 18 June, the main body of the French army arrived at the town of Dieburg, about 20 miles south-west of Aschaffenburg, and it was here that Noailles intended to use the most recent intelligence to make any final adjustments to his plan before committing himself to action. To ascertain the security measures taken by the Allies in order to cover their advance, a division of two brigades of infantry (La Marine and Brancas), supported by a detachment of mounted troops, was sent towards Aschaffenburg under the command of Noailles' nephew, the Duc de Gramont. At the same time, the Brigade Dauphin, under the command of the Comte de Maillebois, was sent even further south to Miltenberg, and the Brigade Irlandaise moved up to Gross-Ostheim, from where it could support either Gramont at Aschaffenburg or operations further south. These marching columns would encounter Allied cavalry patrols as they neared their objectives, and although these were easily swatted aside, each of the opposing army commanders now received his first intelligence as to the enemy presence.

From Dieburg, and ensuring that a screen of cavalry kept any unwanted eyes at bay, Noailles planned to conduct a close and thorough reconnaissance of the towns and villages along the 'French' bank of the Main. The idea was already germinating that if he were able to cut both the Allies' lines of advance and retreat, and combined with their known supply problems, it could force them into a precipitate battle, one which had the potential to neutralize the Pragmatic Army as a fighting force. There were naturally several other rewards that could be reaped as part of such an action, but the veteran soldier chose to ignore them until they became more of a certainty than a possibility.

Deliberately choosing to limit the size of his escort to that of a lower-ranking officer, Noailles spent both 20 and 21 June riding between Seligenstadt in the north and Obernburg in the south, making notes as to the nature of the river at the various towns and villages where he stopped, mapping the location of any known fords and bridges, ascertaining the defensive properties of each of these crossing points and eventually ordering that timber – for bridging materials – be gathered at both Seligenstadt and Niedernberg. By now, the Frenchman had already settled upon the core elements of his plan: he would hit the Allies whilst they were strung out on their line of march, but the main variable would depend upon how fast and in which direction the enemy were marching at that moment in time.

At this stage of his planning, Noailles was content to identify a number of locations along the potential enemy route that, when occupied by French troops, would admirably serve as chokepoints to hinder or even prevent their forward or rearward movement, as circumstances dictated. When the Pragmatic Army moved southwards into the fields above Dettingen, he became certain of the viability of his plan, and immediately gave instructions for the construction of two pontoon bridges at Seligenstadt. His intention was that, when needed, they could be easily swung across the river with the current and quickly anchored on the far bank, thereby allowing a large body of troops to cross the river and cut the road back to Hanau. Similar instructions were given for the construction of a single bridge at Niedernberg. In light of the events of the next few days, this may, at first glance, seem to be an unnecessary step for the marshal to have taken; but not only did it maintain the flexibility of his overall plan by giving him another tactical option, it would also give the Allies something more to think about once the trap was about to be sprung. However, and as if to emphasize how his plan was developing, Noailles gave orders on 24 June for the Brigade d'Orléans, together with a battery of eight cannon, to occupy Seligenstadt and place it in a state of military defence. A natural consequence of these deployments was that the French would be able to interfere with Allied attempts to resupply themselves via the Main River, forcing the enemy to rely on the single road from Hanau.

The following day, and as the main body moved towards the town of Stockstadt, he sent the Duc d'Estrées northwards to Seligenstadt with a force consisting of the infantry brigades Touraine and Auvergne, together with the Brigade des Carabiniers, the Brigade de France-Royal cavalry, the Brigade de Bauffremont (dragoons) and a battery of artillery, the whole force comprising ten battalions of infantry, 26 squadrons of cavalry and eight guns. In addition, the Gardes Françaises and the Brigade Noailles Infanterie were temporarily thrown across the Main to create a fortified bridgehead at Stockstadt and cover the main body of the army; both of these formations would, over the course of the next few days, be relocated to Seligenstadt, with their place in the front line being taken over by other infantry brigades.

Finally, and in perhaps the most crucial of all of these deployments, Noailles now gave orders for the siting of five concealed batteries of heavy artillery between Mainflingen and Stockstadt, their task being to take the enemy columns in enfilade once battle had been joined.

# THE ALLIES AT BAY

Having moved to the right bank of the Main in order to avoid their superior enemy, the Allied commanders had to all intents and purposes placed a logistical noose around their own necks: a single road, and lack of adequate wheeled transport, meant that much of their supplies would need to be transported by river. This would be a hazardous undertaking at the best of times, and a most dangerous one when only one bank of the waterway, which would be used to ship the precious cargo, was controlled.

With the intention being for the Pragmatic Army to continue with its march into Upper Bavaria in order to link up with the forces of Prince Charles of Lorraine, the Earl of Stair's initial plan was to continue south as far as Aschaffenburg and there await the arrival of King George II, who was at that time en route from Hanover. The delay would naturally serve to both rest the troops and give them an opportunity to improve their supply situation through foraging. Accordingly, a combined force of horse and foot, under the command of Lieutenant-General Jasper Clayton, was thrown out ahead of the marching columns, with orders to move independently of the main body and secure the all-important bridge at Aschaffenburg, without which the entire Allied plan of campaign would simply grind to an ignominious halt.

During 16 June, the rest of the army was to come up, following in Clayton's wake. Leading the column, the British (under Stair) were to camp around Aschaffenburg, followed by the Hanoverians under Georg Friedrich von Sommerfeld, who established their headquarters at Mainaschaff; the Austrians, under Arenberg, brought up the rear, and pitched their tents around Klein-Ostheim – the distance between the army commander and his deputy being some six miles. Finally, the rearmost element of the army was a detachment of Austrian dragoons under O'Donnel, whose task was to occupy the village of Dettingen and maintain the road link with Hanau.

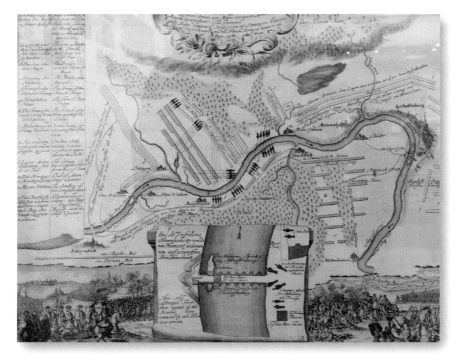

A watercolour map of the Battle of Dettingen. Of particular interest is the inset showing the stone bridge at Aschaffenburg.

Flanked by the water-meadows stretching down to the Main on one side and fields crowned with green, ripening corn on the other, the army began setting up its encampments.

We are uncertain as to the exact route that the Allies had intended to follow in the event of a further march into Upper Bavaria. The army could have crossed the Main at Aschaffenburg, thus availing itself of an arguably better road; or alternately, it could have continued to travel on the eastern bank of the river, a course which would have made for slower going, but one that would have been more shielded from enemy attack.

Despite this lack of information, and given that the Allies were obviously planning on remaining encamped at this location for the next few days, they inexplicably mounted no immediate attempt to secure either the far end of the Aschaffenburg Bridge or the town of Stockstadt, which lay on the opposite side of the Main from the Hanoverian encampment. These omissions would have significant influence upon the next stages in the Allied plan of campaign. In terms of movement, the complete possession of the bridge at Aschaffenburg would have guaranteed the army's continued progress, whilst in purely military terms, the establishment of bridgeheads at Aschaffenburg and Stockstadt would have greatly increased the security of the Allied columns, thus restricting the enemy's options as to dictating how and where any battle would be fought.

Indeed, and as events would come to show, Noailles had already seen the potential of both sites, and these would figure prominently in his final planning. In fact, when Stair led a body of 300 cavalry across the Main in order to reconnoitre the woodland south of Aschaffenburg, his force was so roughly handled by the enemy that the earl suffered the ignominy of being wounded and nearly captured before pulling his troops back to safety. This aborted reconnaissance had, however, achieved its primary objective: of the two possible routes forward, Stair now knew that one of them was firmly blocked by the enemy. With the far end of the bridge clearly in enemy hands, a frontal assault across the causeway would undoubtedly be a bloody affair, and whilst the Allies could bridge the river with the intent of flanking the French position, such a construction would take time – and it was becoming clear that this was a commodity as precious as either food or ammunition.

The problem for the Scotsman was that if he ordered the army to continue its march along the eastern bank of the Main, it would be outflanked and the enemy granted egress into its rear as soon as the troops had passed either Mainaschaff or Aschaffenburg. The immediate effect of the latter would be that the road to Hanau – its sole line of communication and supply – would be immediately and irrevocably cut. Most of the options available to him were unpalatable to say the least, and it was with some relief, no doubt, that he reflected upon the impending arrival of a higher authority.

For two days, the army remained in position, with patrols and vedettes giving increasing warning of the presence of growing numbers of French troops on the far side of the Main. Then, on the morning of 19 June, as the troops went through their daily routine, a convoy of over a hundred wagons, carts and carriages began to thread its way through the Austrian and Hanoverian encampments, before finally halting at the Earl of Stair's field headquarters. Aboard were John, Lord Carteret (the king's close friend and advisor); William Augustus, Duke of Cumberland (the king's second, but favourite, son); and naturally the man whose presence would now relegate

Stair's role to that of a senior officer rather than the commanding general – George Augustus, Duke of Brunswick-Lüneburg, Electoral Prince of Hanover and – above all of these – King of England.

The Main at Aschaffenburg. At the time of the battle, the river was wider and shallower, but the water level was about 10ft higher.

If any of the army's senior officers were inclined to believe that the king's arrival would serve to instil a new dynamism, a new energy, into the army's conduct, they would not have long to wait before they were painfully disabused of the notion. Indeed, the only real effect of the royal advent was a dangerous splintering of the command structure. Whereas previously, Stair had been first among equals and therefore had the final say in any decision-making, it can easily be asserted that now, and at this crucial juncture, despite being the commander of the largest contingent within the army, he did not even have that. The Hanoverian generals led by von Sommerfeld sought to refer any concerns directly to their sovereign, instead of following the established chain of command; whilst one of the two Austrian field marshals – von Neipperg – felt that his personal connections at the Hofburg in Vienna granted him the leeway to make unofficial 'suggestions' at the highest levels.

Over the course of the following week, the Allies chose to remain supine, failing to undertake even the simplest of operations to deflect the enemy from their purpose. Instead, they remained stationary as French forces secured Stockstadt and naturally enough established a strong bridgehead on the right bank of the Main. With these and the other troop movements that Noailles had previously set in train towards Seligenstadt, Miltenberg and Niedernberg, the French had effectively cut enemy access to the river, and, as a result, the future and continued existence of the Pragmatic Army hung from a single thread: the Hanau–Aschaffenburg road. Were this to be cut, the army would, in all likelihood, be forced to surrender through lack of adequate supply.

With his plan drawing inexorably ever closer to its culmination, Noailles was by now more than content to surrender the initiative to his opponents. He had them where he wanted them, and whether the Pragmatic Army attempted to continue its southward march or instead retraced its footsteps towards Hanau, the central core of his plan remained valid and would deliver certain victory over the enemy. And yet, the question must be asked: even at this late stage, was there anything that the Allies still could have done, any course of action that they could have pursued, which would have delivered them from the precarious situation in which they currently found themselves?

The answer is, unfortunately, a resounding 'no'.

In the warm afterglow following the battle, many of Stair's detractors would accuse him of having blindly led the army into a trap, from which it was only extricated by the bravery and military acumen of King George. Yet with Noailles' army in close proximity, there was nothing else he could do other than to choose a suitable position and await the king's safe arrival. Had he chosen to continue with the advance into Upper Bavaria, both the army and the royal party would still have needed to negotiate enemy-occupied

The Episcopal Palace of the Schloss Johannisburg, which housed the British headquarters prior to the battle.

territory until it was able to unite with Prince Charles in Bavaria. On 19 June, when he formally handed over command of the army to his king, he naturally handed over the responsibility for its direction. This now resided with the king, who possessed what he had desired for some time: the opportunity to demonstrate that he was as able a *Feldherr* as his nephew, Frederick of Prussia.

It was an inauspicious start to this new phase of the campaign: for almost a week, the new commander-in-chief made no decisions, and gave no orders. During daylight hours, activity on the French side of the river could easily be observed from church spires, and a number of contemporary accounts of the battle would further have the reader believe that the two pontoon bridges below Gross-Welzheim had been swung across the Main and anchored on the Allied bank of the river before the day of the battle. But even if the latter had not actually been the case, it would have been clear to any officer of experience that something was afoot, that the French were in the final stages of preparation for whatever operation Noailles had planned.

It was late in the evening of 26 June, and with the Pragmatic Army still stretched out in its various bivouacs and encampments, when – having previously summoned the army's senior officers to a council of war – King George used the interim to meet with Carteret, Stair and Cumberland at his headquarters in the Schloss Johannisburg to discuss the army's situation.

Those present were more than aware that the failure to secure the southern end of the stone bridge at Aschaffenburg had effectively removed any realistic possibility of a union with the imperial forces in Upper Bavaria. The only other option open to the Pragmatic Army would be to follow the meandering course of the Main along its northern bank, denuding its strength by leaving garrisons at the various crossing points in order to delay any enemy pursuit. But, and until the troops had travelled far enough so as to be able to draw upon the Austrian magazines in Bavaria, each step would not only be one further from their own source of supply, but would also increase the ability of the enemy to cut this most precarious of links. All were naturally in favour of what they saw to be the only realistic course of action remaining open to them: a return to Hanau, where the army could rest, refit and resupply.

The problem was that although he was the king of Great Britain, George was not present as such, but rather as Elector of Hanover. His troops – whether British or Hanoverian – were not there as allies, but instead as subsidiaries hired by contract. There was therefore a fine and almost invisible line between his being able to dictate policy and his being able to influence it. All that could be done was to persuade the council of war to make a decision by consensus, one that would naturally reflect the conclusion that the British high command had just reached.

Eventually calling the meeting to order, and with a dozen or so general officers present, Stair summarized the current situation. Firstly, and irrespective of either the enemy presence astride the main road from Aschaffenburg or the bridgehead at Stockstadt, the Duc de Noailles was known to be somewhere on the western bank of the Main River at the head of a French army estimated to be in the region of 70,000 men, a force which comfortably outnumbered the Allied forces. Secondly, and although the army had recently been fully resupplied from the magazine at Hanau, with the river now cut by the enemy, the future movement of supplies was now limited to that which could be sent by road.

The Water Gate, at the Schloss Johanissburg, Aschaffenburg. In 1743, the Main River would have flowed under the arch.

In short, although ammunition remained plentiful, the troops were actually consuming food faster than it could be received. The depth of the irony was that whilst the army was surrounded by fields sown with wheat, the crops themselves were unripe and were not due to be harvested for some months. The only option had therefore been to place the troops on reduced rations, but this could only be a short-term solution, a temporary respite from a potential disaster. Even now, the provosts had begun reporting instances of theft and desertion, the latter being a potential source of intelligence for the Duc de Noailles, whose troops had no logistical problems whatsoever. The Allies, therefore, had to change their position and improve their own supply situation. The question was: Where should they move to?

Arenberg, as the army's nominal second-in-command, now rose to address the meeting. It was clear that he intended to reiterate his position: the decision for a junction to be made with Prince Charles had been taken at the highest of levels, and a failure to meet this agreement would naturally compromise the Allied campaign in Bavaria. What was unclear to those present was whether or not he would choose to address what in modern parlance would be referred to as the elephant in the room. In other words, the delay which had enabled the French to catch up with the Pragmatic Army was in fact the very same amount of time that had been spent waiting for King George to conclude his personal business in Hanover and join the army; that almost half of the wheeled transport currently with the army was engaged in the carriage of the royal suite; and finally, that the presence of the king's entourage – both in terms of personnel and animals – had tipped the army's supply situation into its current dangerous imbalance.

In the event, and having made his point on behalf of the Austrian government, Arenberg sat down. Several of those present were then asked for their advice. Naturally enough, the British generals endorsed Stair's summary of the situation, and one can only assume that the Hanoverians present – as auxiliaries of the British crown – followed suit. As a sovereign monarch, King George had the final word, and announced the decision that had been made in camera before the council of war had even begun: in the best interests of the army, it would conduct an immediate withdrawal to Hanau. Accordingly, orders were then drafted to the effect that the army was to sleep that evening 'under arms', and that the troops would be 'stood to' some hours before dawn the following morning in order that the men could begin their march with the least amount of delay.

It was at this point that the king made the first of several errors that would characterize the battle, when he stated that the British contingent would occupy the post of honour and would lead the army during the march.

The problem was that, having previously led the advance from Hanau to Aschaffenburg, the commanders of the British contingent now found themselves in the worst possible position. The British – as the army's vanguard – were actually the contingent furthest away from the new objective, and in order for them to comply with the royal directive, they would need to march through the Hanoverian and Austrian encampments before they could assume their place at the head of the column.

Given that the immediate objective was to simply get the troops across the morass watered by the Forchbach and into the open fields beyond Dettingen, the most sensible – and indeed most logical – course of action would have been for the army to reverse its order of march, with the Austrians leading off, followed by the Hanoverians and then the British; the army would then reorganize itself somewhere between the villages of Dettingen and Hörstein once the adverse terrain had been safely negotiated. Adherence to the king's pronouncement, however, meant that first the Hanoverian and then the Austrian troops would need to leave the roadway, and then – once the British had passed – rejoin the column in sequence.

The scale of the error can be shown in the fact that the British at Aschaffenburg were actually some nine miles from their initial objective, whilst the Austrians around Kleinostheim were but three miles distant. This would have meant that Austrian troops could realistically have been in possession of Dettingen relatively early in the morning of 27 June, thus ensuring a secure crossing point for the rest of the army, instead of using this time to vacate the road and clear a passage for their British allies. In making his decision, King George had committed the most basic of errors by failing to consider that Noailles would be following his own plan of campaign, rather than reacting to any enemy movement; and by assuming that, having effectively manoeuvred the Pragmatic Army into its current position, Noailles would allow it to march unmolested out of the trap that he had set for it.

As the debate continued, it was pointed out that – bordered by the Main River to the west, the Spessart Hills to the east, the Aschaff River to the south and the Forchbach to the north – the army was in fact caught in a potentially lethal box, in which the Allies could easily be forced into an engagement on unfavourable terms. Conceding to this danger, the high command agreed that instead of a single column marching along the road, the army would now march in two wings – led by the Duke of Arenberg and the Earl of Stair respectively. The first, and larger, of these wings (consisting of almost all the cavalry, the artillery and wheeled transport, together with the bulk of the infantry) would follow the road and use the crossing at Dettingen; whilst the remainder of the army (almost totally infantry) would march cross-country through the wheat fields and the lower, wooded, slopes of the Spessart Hills in order to make a crossing at the second causeway, further to the east.

One thing that marred this rather radical departure from normal procedure was King George's continued insistence that his redcoats should, and indeed would, still lead the van. In effect, this meant that within the column designated as coming under Arenberg's command, those units closest to the initial objective, i.e. the Austrians, would still need to move off the road in order to allow the British to pass; and then – once they and any Hanoverian troops had done so – reassume their place in the column. Once the army had gotten underway and Dettingen had been secured, the baggage train would follow the left wing, in turn being followed by the rear-guard, whose task was to prevent any interference from the French troops at Stockstadt and Aschaffenburg.

The generals then retired to their own headquarters, to issue brigade orders and prepare for the following day's march, fully unaware that the coming day would turn out fundamentally different to anything that any of them could have anticipated.

Sometime around 6.00am, the Austrian outposts covering Gross-Welzheim were alerted by noises coming from the far side of the river. O'Donnel was immediately informed, and when he came up to investigate for himself, he was able to make out a significant body of enemy troops massing on the far bank. Even as he watched, a column of brightly attired horsemen drove their horses into the shallows and began to swim them across the river.

It was obvious that this was the first stage in an enemy movement to establish a further bridgehead on the eastern bank of the Main, a lodgement whose only possible objective was to capture Dettingen and thereby cut the Hanau road. Without needing to calculate the odds stacked against him, the Irishman scribbled a hasty note to Arenberg to inform his superior of the enemy activity, adding as a postscript the news that he would be abandoning Dettingen, as its defence was – in his professional judgement – no longer tenable.

As the messenger sped off, threading his way through the mass of the army, O'Donnel dictated a series of notes to one of his aides-de-camp, fully aware that the accuracy of any information that he could provide Arenberg with would be a key factor in the development of the Allied response to the presence of enemy troops to their rear.

The situation now facing the leaders of the Pragmatic Army had the undertones of a worst-case scenario. With the army suffering from a lack of supply, and with the road now effectively blocked in both directions, it was clear that the troops would be immediately forming up for battle on very unfavourable terrain, rather than for a normal day's march.

The most effective course of action that the Allies could have pursued at this stage would have been to simply abandon the planned march deployment and then reverse the normal line of battle. Although this would have meant that those troops normally allocated to the left of the line would have occupied the right and vice versa, it would have ensured that those troops closest to the enemy would still have had a reasonable chance of being able to engage or contain the French bridgehead before it could be exploited, and thus cover the movement of the army's left flank. Even if the village of Dettingen had by this stage fallen to the French, with competent officers such a manoeuvre could have been achieved relatively easily, and could have facilitated the army's deployment for battle. However, it was at this point that King George demonstrated that he clearly lacked the military acumen of his famed nephew Frederick, when he reiterated that the British would occupy the 'position of honour' on the right of the line of battle, despite the fact that the British contingent was now divided between the two manoeuvre columns. The king himself would, initially at least, remain with the rear-guard.

Musket balls recovered from the battlefield of Dettingen.

The most likely result of this royal declaration would ultimately have been a completely unbalanced battlefield deployment. If King George's instructions had been followed to the letter, and in order to reach their position in the line of battle, the British would have been obliged to march through their allies' encampments, with the (by then undoubtedly disordered) Hanoverians following suit and marching through the Austrian contingent in order to reach their place in the line. Only then would the brigade commanders be able to issue the orders that would see the battalions and squadrons form up for battle. Given that the instructions being issued from the army headquarters were being constantly overtaken by reports of enemy movements, we can only speculate as to the effect that these proposed manoeuvres would have had on the Hapsburg contingent; at the bottom line, they would certainly have rendered them *hors de combat* for several crucial hours.

Whilst the left wing resolved its problems, the right wing – under Stair – left the road, angling towards the easternmost causeway. Leading off with a brigade of four British battalions (Handasyde, Charles Howard, Huske, Royal North British Fusiliers), followed by a similar-sized force of Hanoverians (Wrangel, Soubiron, Borch, Schulenberg), the infantry trudged slowly through the wheat fields, their progress crushing the crops underfoot, so that their supporting brigade of Hanoverian dragoons (Pontpietin, Bussche, Adlepsen, Wendt), together with a battery of Hanoverian artillery, had a much easier time of it.

With its troops ultimately forming both the centre and the left flank of the Allied battle line, the exact progress of the left wing is much more difficult to gauge, and as a result must be tempered by an inevitable amount of conjecture. To the east of the road, the fields were, as we have seen, covered with ripening crops, which (if we study accounts of the Battle of Quatre Bras, which took place in Belgium almost exactly 72 years later) would have more than likely reached to the chests of any troops on foot marching through them. The road itself – a spur of the Alte Heer und Handelstrasse, which crossed the Main near Seligenstadt – separated the fields from the water-meadows that stretched down to the Main.

The most likely sequence of events is that when the French troops finally came into view, and instead of simply pulling his troops aside so as to let the British cavalry pass, Arenberg consciously moved them eastwards into the fields. From here, they could not only protect the cavalry's right flank, but could also link up with the troops of the right wing, thus ensuring the integrity of the battle line. Two brigades of Austrian foot were deployed in such a manner (de Ligne, Los Rios, Prié and a battalion of the Wolfenbüttel infantry in the first line, with Arenberg, Gaisrück and the second battalion of Wolfenbüttel supporting them as a second line). With the space created by the previous manoeuvres, a six-battalion British brigade (Thomas Howard, Johnson, Rothes, Duroure, Onslow and Pulteney) was then slotted in as the third line of the centre, and finally a converged Anglo-Austrian brigade (Arenberg, Salm, Heister, Welsh Fuzileers and Ponsonby) took up position as the fourth and final line of troops in the centre.

With Arenberg taking responsibility for the centre, command of the left wing of the army technically fell upon Cumberland's shoulders, ably seconded by Sir Philip Honywood as the Earl of Stair's ranking deputy. Having successfully negotiated their way through the Allied encampments, the British horsemen now occupied the head of the army's left flank, their lines stretching from the road to the meadows leading down to the Main. First in line stood the cream of the British cavalry (Bland, Somerset, Life Guards, Stair and Hawley), closely supported by the regiments of Ligonier, Honywood, Rich and Cope. Immediately behind the British cavalry came a brigade of five Hanoverian battalions (Monroy, Zastrow, Böselager, Middachten and Sommerfeld), followed by three further lines of Allied cavalry. The fourth line comprised two regiments of Hanoverian horse (Bremer and Schultzen) paired with two of Austrian dragoons (Lüneburg-Styrum and de Ligne). Behind these, the fifth and sixth lines of troops each mustered a brigade of Hanoverian heavy cavalry: the Leibregiment zu Pferd, Wrede and Hammerstein, followed by the Garde Grenadiere zu Pferd, the Gardes du Corps, Montigny and Bülow.

The fact that the Allied left was six lines deep, as opposed to four lines in the centre and three lines on the right flank, especially when considering that five out of six available cavalry brigades were deployed on this flank, gives ample testament to the constricted nature of the battlefield. Quite simply, the entire area east of the road was unsuitable for mounted troops. This also gives us an indication of the relative ad hoc nature of the Allied deployment: Monroy's brigade of infantry was directly in the middle of a cavalry wing, with two brigades to their front and three to their rear, with nowhere for the troops to their front to rally, should the necessity arise, and nowhere for the troops behind them to deploy for battle if needed. In effect, the placement of Monroy's brigade was another example of how Noailles' plan had discomfited his opponents.

Next in sequence came the artillery, the batteries slowly filing into position, ready to provide close fire support as and when needed. The exact deployment of the various batteries remains uncertain, but from later accounts we can be certain that at least one Hanoverian battery was placed on the right, the Austrian guns were placed in the centre, and at least one British battery would support the left of the army, ultimately being drawn into an unequal counter-battery engagement against the French heavy artillery.

Finally came the rear-guard, whose instructions were to forestall any enemy pursuit from either Aschaffenburg or Stockstadt, comprising both the British and Hanoverian Foot Guards – three and two battalions respectively – together with two battalions of Hanoverian foot (Campe, Jung-Spörken) and the Royal North British Dragoons.

At this stage the army had been stood to for some hours and, apart from the troops under the Earl of Stair, little progress had been made towards attaining the objectives agreed upon at the earlier council of war. But now, reports began to filter back from the leading elements that enemy troops had been spotted moving in and around Dettingen. It was clear to all that battle would soon be joined, and that in order to reach safety, the army would need to bludgeon its way across the Forchbach and sweep aside the enemy troops barring their way. Thanks to O'Donnel's prescience, the Allied commanders already had a rough idea of the size and composition of the force facing them. However, given the nature of the terrain ahead, they would have no concrete idea as to its exact numbers or dispositions until shortly before the moment of contact.

Their only option would be to complete their own deployments and then give the order to advance. As part of the former, orders were given that the baggage train – together with King George's suite – was to leave the road and strike eastwards along a little-used track towards the Spessart Hills, removing the danger of it being caught up in the middle of a pitched battle, whilst ensuring that the right wing of the army was in a position to prevent their being targeted by enemy troops. Once the wagons were under way, the order was given to continue the advance.

# CHECKMATE?

Over the previous days, as he had patiently waited for the Allies to hold their councils of war and then make their move, Noailles had been receiving constant intelligence reports. These came not only from his patrols, but also from Allied soldiers who had been captured, or who – with their rations severely cut – had attempted to give themselves up in the hope of receiving warm and plentiful food as prisoners of war.

At 1.00am on 27 June, he withdrew both the Gardes Françaises and the Noailles Infanterie from Stockstadt, ordering them to join those forces already assembled at Seligenstadt for the crossing of the Main. Similar orders were then given to the elite of the elite, the cavalry of the Maison Militaire du Roi, His Most Christian Majesty's household troops. As dawn broke, the marshal gave orders for the advance elements of the cavalry to begin their crossing. The Brigade de Bauffremont Dragons crossed by the fords at Gross-Welzheim, whilst two regiments of hussars under the Marquis de Berchény would swim their horses across the river, and then, upon reaching the far bank, seize Dettingen itself, a mile or so distant. The troops designated to strike the first blow in the coming battle comprised, ironically enough, a force whose core was a body of expatriate Hungarians in rebellion against the regime of the woman officially referred to by their commanders as neither empress nor archduchess, but rather as Queen of Hungary.

Once these two objectives had been taken, the lower ends of both pontoon bridges would then be cut loose from their moorings, so that the river current could carry them to the far bank, where they would be secured. Led by the Duc de Noailles in person, the infantry and artillery would then use the two bridges to cross the Main with the cavalry moving across via the fords. All told, some 30,000 men drawn from some of the army's most prestigious regiments would make the crossing, their shared lineages reflecting the trust which Noailles had placed in them. Once the troops were safely across the river, a brigade of foot was to remain behind to cover the new bridgehead; the main body would move up to Berchény's position, where they would deploy for battle, covered by the defiles and the marshy terrain watered by the Forchbach and Hoggräben – and there they would await the enemy's approach.

As the troops advanced to their allotted positions, Noailles summoned the various divisional commanders and senior officers to a final impromptu council of war. As the men gathered, he reminded them that theirs was to be a blocking force, and that its sole objective was to prevent the enemy from breaking through and continuing its march on Hanau. They were to be an obstacle that the Allies could not bypass, an anvil upon which the enemy army would be hammered and ultimately broken.

## The battle deployment, according to British sources

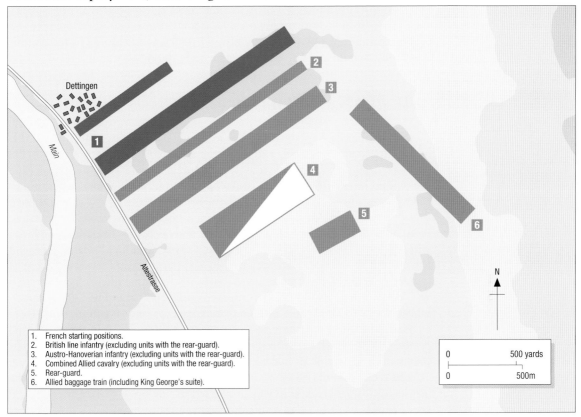

Dettingen

Main

Altestrasse

N

1. French starting positions.
2. British line infantry (excluding units with the rear-guard).
3. Austro-Hanoverian infantry (excluding units with the rear-guard).
4. Combined Allied cavalry (excluding units with the rear-guard).
5. Rear-guard.
6. Allied baggage train (including King George's suite).

| 0 | | 500 yards |
| 0 | | 500m |

Openly admitting that he had originally intended to command this force in person, Noailles concluded by saying that his presence was required at his field headquarters at Stockstadt, so that he could ensure that all interlocking elements of his plan would come together at their allotted times. As a result, the blocking force was now to come under the direct command of his nephew, the Duc de Gramont, Colonel of the Gardes Françaises. Strictly speaking, Noailles' assertion was not entirely accurate, as his headquarters staff contained several experienced officers of general rank who were more than capable of assuming the responsibility and acting in his stead. Ultimately, this failure or unwillingness to delegate would have nigh-on fatal consequences for his plan of operations.

Gramont's force was therefore ordered to deploy some distance back from the stream, the gap affording some protection from enemy artillery, by preventing it from engaging the Frenchmen at short range, whilst his own cannon were to be positioned so that they could easily cover the causeways across the Forchbach, crossing points which would be raked by a storm of close-range cannister fire as the Allies' leading elements made their way through the marshy terrain. Disordered, the enemy were then to be thrown back by a series of local counter-attacks made *á la baïonette*. This deadly combination of cannister and cold steel would ensure that they would fail in any attempts to break through towards Hanau and thus allow the other facets of Noailles' plan to slot into place and ensure a French victory.

An aide brought Noailles his horse, and as he mounted, he turned to the coterie of officers and asked them again if they understood their orders. With their affirmation ringing in his ears, he signalled to his staff and escort, and spurred his mount towards the pontoon bridges, secure in the belief that his battle plan would develop exactly as he had envisaged.

## THE PLAN UNFOLDS

It was probably approaching 9.00am when Noailles returned to his headquarters at Stockstadt, and whilst he ate a light breakfast, he dictated a series of orders. The first of these was to the Prince de Tingry commanding the two infantry brigades south of Aschaffenburg; Noailles instructed him to throw a detachment of troops across the bridge, and once it was ascertained that the enemy were fully committed to their northwards march, he was then to occupy the town and there await the arrival of the Brigade Irlandaise, which was already moving up from Gross-Ostheim. Once the Irishmen had arrived, the combined force was to advance parallel to Stockstadt, where it would be joined by the two brigades currently manning the bridgehead. This would give Tingry some 22 battalions of infantry – roughly 14,000 men – whose principal task would be then to deploy across the Hanau road and form a second line of French bayonets. This would further hem in the Pragmatic Army and block its line of retreat when the Allies inevitably accepted that they would be unable to make any forward progress at Dettingen.

The second set of orders went, naturally enough, to the commander at the Stockstadt bridgehead, who was instructed to link up with Tingry. The final set of orders went to de la Vallière, overseeing the concealed heavy artillery batteries: when the signal to open fire was given, he was to directly engage the open flank of the enemy columns – which would, at that stage, be milling about before the Forchbach – and to keep firing at them until either his guns overheated or his powder and ammunition had run out.

Everything was now either in place or moving into place. The enemy would soon find an immovable object blocking their way forward, and a similar one blocking their route backward. They could not negotiate the Spessart Hills as an army, nor could they cross the Main and attack Noailles' main body on the far side of the river without access to a suitable crossing point. Furthermore, the advance of the Prince de Tingry would soon remove from the equation the only reasonable option available to them: the bridge at Stockstadt. Unable to advance or retreat, to move left or right, the Allies would soon be reduced to the choice of two possible options: surrender or die. His Most Christian Majesty's army stood on the cusp of a most famous and single victory, and – if he understandably permitted himself a small moment of hubris – Noailles was certain that all eventualities had been considered and catered for. All that he needed to do now was to prepare the announcement of victory that would soon be sent to his royal master at Versailles.

## THE PLAN UNRAVELS

According to his testimony after the battle, the Duc de Gramont – on scanning the enemy ranks through his telescope – saw not an army advancing

The fateful order: the Duc de Gramont is seen handing a dispatch to a waiting officer. Whether it is the order to attack or withdraw can only be speculated.

resolutely forward and intent on giving battle, but instead one milling in abject disorder, preparing to retreat and likely to flee at the slightest provocation. In short, he saw the same victory to be within his grasp as had his uncle; but in his vision, it was one that would be won at the thrust of a sword or the point of a bayonet, rather than by skilful deployment and planning. In the duke's opinion, a single decisive and overwhelming hammer blow would shatter the Allied army, gaining honour and glory for all those present who took part in the fighting. Instead of waiting defensively for the Pragmatic Army to come to him, he would therefore leave his current position and go over to the attack.

Summoning his divisional commanders to his side, Gramont outlined his intentions. Despite the exhortations of their commander-in-chief of but a short while before, he now urged their acquiescence to a radical change of plan, one that would cover those present with glory. It would appear that this agreement was universally forthcoming, most likely as their backgrounds, and their aspirations, were reflections of his own. Amongst those present were Gramont's cousins (and the marshal's two sons), the Duc d'Ayen and the Comte de Noailles; the Prince de Dombes, the Duc de Penthièvre and the Comte d'Eu, all grandsons of King Louis XIV; the Duc de Chartres, who was both grandson and great-nephew to the Sun King; the Duc de Biron, Gramont's brother-in-law, who commanded on the left flank, and the Duc d'Harcourt, who commanded on the right; the Prince de Soubise, scion of the great family of Rohan; Montesson, the septuagenarian commander of the Maison du Roi; and the youthful Duc de Rochechouart, commander of a regiment of infantry. None of them chose to gainsay their senior officer.

The logistical quandary that Gramont had elected to face was exactly the same as faced by his opponent, albeit in a mirrored fashion: to achieve his aim, he now had to get his troops over the Forchbach and into line of battle before the enemy could conceivably interfere with his deployment. Like

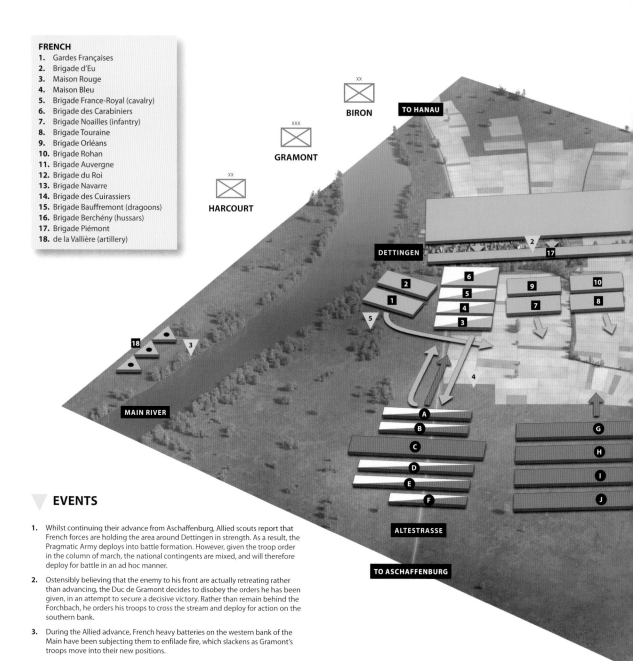

**FRENCH**

1. Gardes Françaises
2. Brigade d'Eu
3. Maison Rouge
4. Maison Bleu
5. Brigade France-Royal (cavalry)
6. Brigade des Carabiniers
7. Brigade Noailles (infantry)
8. Brigade Touraine
9. Brigade Orléans
10. Brigade Rohan
11. Brigade Auvergne
12. Brigade du Roi
13. Brigade Navarre
14. Brigade des Cuirassiers
15. Brigade Bauffremont (dragoons)
16. Brigade Berchény (hussars)
17. Brigade Piémont
18. de la Vallière (artillery)

BIRON

TO HANAU

GRAMONT

HARCOURT

DETTINGEN

MAIN RIVER

ALTESTRASSE

TO ASCHAFFENBURG

## ▼ EVENTS

1. Whilst continuing their advance from Aschaffenburg, Allied scouts report that French forces are holding the area around Dettingen in strength. As a result, the Pragmatic Army deploys into battle formation. However, given the troop order in the column of march, the national contingents are mixed, and will therefore deploy for battle in an ad hoc manner.

2. Ostensibly believing that the enemy to his front are actually retreating rather than advancing, the Duc de Gramont decides to disobey the orders he has been given, in an attempt to secure a decisive victory. Rather than remain behind the Forchbach, he orders his troops to cross the stream and deploy for action on the southern bank.

3. During the Allied advance, French heavy batteries on the western bank of the Main have been subjecting them to enfilade fire, which slackens as Gramont's troops move into their new positions.

4. In an attempt to defeat the Allied left flank in detail before the main body of either army can engage, the Duc d'Harcourt orders an immediate attack by the French right-wing cavalry. Led by the men of the Maison Rouge (Mousquetaires and Gendarmes), the leading elements of the French cavalry break through, but do not break the two lines of British cavalry, who have ridden forward to meet them. As they ride out of the rear of the British lines, the French guardsmen continue towards the third line of Allied troops (Monroy's Brigade), but rein in, and then retire when faced by a steady line of enemy muskets. Unknown to the cavalrymen, the earlier enfilading fire has hit the brigade's headquarters group, killing both von Monroy and a number of his staff. With its command structure ruptured, the Hanoverian troops are therefore in no state to engage the enemy horsemen to their front, and are more than content to allow the Frenchmen to retire unmolested.

5. Once the French cavalry have launched their attack, the Gardes Françaises execute a wheel on their left flank, so as to put them in a position to threaten the now-open flank of the advancing Allied centre. Whilst they do so, the Brigade d'Eu moves forward to occupy the Gardes' previous position. By doing so, they open up an area behind them, into which the French cavalry can – if required – withdraw in order to reorganize between attacks, protected by the infantry's muskets.

## 'A PLAN UNRAVELLED'
### The opening moves, *c.* 9.30am–11.30am

FORCHBACH

14

15

12    13

16

HOGGRÄBEN

K

L    M

O

N

1

N

KING GEORGE II

CUMBERLAND

ARENBERG

STAIR

**PRAGMATIC ARMY**
A. Campbell
B. Hawley
C. Monroy
D. Pontpiétin
E. Hammerstein
F. Launay
G. Neipperg
H. Chanclos
I. Clayton
J. Salm
K. Howard
L. Wrangel
M. Wendt
N. Ilten
O. Baggage train

Legend has it that the British paychest was lost on the battlefield, and a lonesome redcoat – *der Rotröcke* – spends eternity trying to find it.

them, he was reduced to solely using the two causeways as the banks of the stream; whilst passable to small bodies of men, they still presented a significant obstacle to the movement of troops. We have no written record of the French order of march at this point, but given the contemporary map at the Bibliothèque Nationale de France, we can assume with relative safety that the eastern causeway was initially used by Berchény's hussar brigade, which took station on the extreme left flank of the French line, followed by the infantry brigades of Noailles, Touraine, Auvergne, Roi and Navarre, who – once across – marched west before wheeling successively in order to form the centre and left of the front line of battle. Behind them came the brigade of dragoons, who were to act as a link between the infantry and the light cavalry, and finally the brigade of cuirassiers, armoured cavalrymen whose task now was to ride down the beaten enemy. Once this first line of troops was in place, an eight-gun battery of artillery made its way across the defile, followed by the infantry brigades of Orléans and Rohan, which took up a supporting position behind Auvergne, Touraine and Noailles.

It was on the right flank, however, that the mores of the French aristocracy came to the fore. The troops of the Maison Rouge crossed first: the two troops of red-coated Mousquetaires, followed by the Chevau-légers and Gendarmes de la Garde. Immediately behind came the Maison Bleu, the four companies of the blue-coated Gardes du Corps, brigaded with the Grenadiers à Cheval; each of the Gardes du Corps having a statuary strength of 330 men, thus making each of them almost as large as a regiment of the line. As the cavalrymen deployed astride the road, they were succeeded in the line of march by the battalions of the

A farmhouse on the southern side of the battlefield, at the foot of the Spessart Hills. The lower, lighter brickwork on the building is contemporary to the period of the battle.

Gardes Françaises – Gramont's own regiment – who now moved into position on the right of the Maison, their task being to anchor the extreme right of the French line. To that end they were supported by the Brigade d'Eu Infanterie and a second battery of field artillery, similar in size and composition to that which had crossed via the eastern causeway. Closing the army's right flank and filing into position immediately behind the guard cavalry came the Brigade de France-Royal cavalry and the huge Régiment de Carabiniers – a veritable battering ram of horseflesh whose task would be to smash their way through the enemy ranks and drive them to disaster. With the line of battle now deployed, the remaining formation, the four battalions of the Brigade de Piémont Infanterie, would remain north of the Forchbach, their task – possibly paying lip-service to Noailles' original intention – being to protect the causeway crossings against enemy attack.

A close-up view of crops similar to those covering the field in 1743 – roughly 1.5m in height.

Although it undoubtedly had more to do with the urgency with which the opening phase of Noailles' plan (i.e. the crossing of the Main, the capture of Dettingen and the deployment on the Forchbach) needed to be successfully completed, rather than the actual terrain over which the battle was fought, it should be noted that none of the infantry brigades was served by the battalion guns á la Suédoise that the Chevalier de Malbez, in his account of the campaign, cites as having been attached to them at the commencement of operations. To have manhandled them across the pontoon bridges or through the fords would have been far too time-consuming, and therefore, given that there is no direct mention of their use during the battle, the assumption must be that they were left behind at either Seligenstadt or Stockstadt, the intention being that they would be brought up once the battle had been fought and won.

It was about 8.30am when Gramont's troops began to cross the obstacle that they were in fact supposed to have been defending. It could not have been too long before he was made aware of the fact that his appreciation of the enemy's intentions was quite wrong, and that he was indeed going to have the battle that he had so earnestly desired. However, the latter would not be on the terms that he had anticipated, and he was now forced to make an unenviable decision.

With the crossing of the Forchbach still incomplete, Gramont had only two alternatives open to him. He could firstly countermand his previous orders, recalling those troops that had already made the passage, and revert to Noailles' original plan. As a veteran officer, he knew that a withdrawal in the face of the enemy was a challenging enough manoeuvre, one that had the potential for disaster should the Allies be enterprising enough to launch a cavalry attack straight up the Hanau road with the intent of catching their opponents unprepared as they waited their turn to cross the marshy ground. The second option, and no doubt one that was more palatable to the Frenchman, would be to press on with the deployment regardless of the proximity of the enemy. After all – and as he belatedly found out – whilst his forces now had the Forchbach to their rear, the infantry of the centre still had the Hoggräben stream directly to their front. The stream provided some defensive value as the armies closed.

This was indeed the course of action that Gramont chose to follow, secure in the knowledge that the main body of the Allied army had already encountered the problems caused by the unharvested fields, and that unless something were to go seriously awry, he would have more than sufficient time to complete his dispositions. What he failed to take adequate account of was that the two streams covered his centre to the front, to the rear and to the right flank. This meant that should the troops need to manoeuvre in a hurry, the only feasible direction in which to do so was eastwards. Furthermore, in the event of a withdrawal, he had effectively committed over three-quarters of his army to a single causeway, and the one furthest away from the pontoon bridges at Gross-Welzheim. If his plans were to go awry, it could indeed spell the destruction of his entire command.

What followed was therefore a curious amalgam of the original French plan and a reactive one based upon Gramont's own instincts. The French would continue with their new deployment, but instead of advancing further across the broken terrain to engage the approaching foe, they would simply hold their new positions, allowing the two batteries of field artillery to play upon the Allied ranks, whilst the heavy artillery across the Main at Mainflingen would as planned engage them from the flank.

Faced by such overwhelming firepower, it was inevitable that the Pragmatic Army would falter in its advance. When it did, he would no longer hold his troops in check, and instead would take to the offensive, driving them south onto the bayonets of Tingry's advancing brigades.

## THE DIE IS CAST

The time was now approaching 11.00am, and as the two armies made their final deployments, staff officers on both sides moved to positions from which they could gain a clearer view of their opponents, not only to ascertain the numbers ranged against them, but also – given certain differences in uniform – to gain an appreciation as to where certain troops might be deployed. If Gramont's staff, for example, were able to pick out enemy troops in white coats, they would naturally be Austrian, or if in red either British or Hanoverian. Conversely, few regiments of the French army were clothed in dark blue coats, and of those only one such unit comprised several battalions; so if the Allied staff were able to locate a significant body of infantry in such a shade of blue, they would in all probability have been able to locate the position of the Gardes Françaises, regarded by many as being the elite of His Most Christian Majesty's foot troops.

As couriers rode between the formations, delivering the brigadiers' final instructions, and by now having left the rear-guard under the command of the Hanoverian lieutenant-general Thomas von Ilten, King George now rode up to the head of the Allied right wing, intent on joining the Earl of Stair and directing the battle from that position. As the king approached Stair's

headquarters, his horse shied and bolted. The monarch's dignity – and no doubt his person – was saved by Ensign Cyrus Trapaud of Charles Howard's regiment of foot, who reputedly caught the animal and held it long enough for the king to dismount safely.[9] With his charger seemingly calmed, and his feet on firm ground, King George was apparently asked if he would care to remount. The royal response, which we would need to treat as being apocryphal rather than actual, was in the negative, being later reported as 'I don't need a damned horse!' After the battle, this apparent show of bravado was to gain much currency at home and abroad as being the sign of a warrior-king, a role which King George had actively sought. King George then strode through the ranks of British infantry. When there was nothing between him and the French lines but open fields, he drew his sword, and taking position as any gentleman would at his *salle d'armes*, pointed his weapon at the enemy ranks and called out the order to march. At this point, the battalion drummers began to beat the tempo, and as this staccato tattoo rippled down the line, the Pragmatic Army stepped off and began its advance.

The problem with this anecdote is that chroniclers of the battle have made the assumption that King George actually fought the battle on foot. Given that the purpose of being mounted is not just for speed of movement but also for elevation and visibility, without the latter a commander is unable to command in an effective manner: he cannot see and conversely cannot be seen, affecting the constant flow of information that influences the decisions made and orders given during the course of a battle.

In social terms, it would have meant that if the king were on foot, then his staff would have had to dismount as well. This would have inhibited their

This evocative painting by Ernest Crofts, RA shows King George II leading his troops into battle. Dettingen itself is juxtaposed from the left to the right of the battlefield.

9   As a reward for his quick thinking, Trapaud was given a lieutenant's commission. He would end his career almost 60 years later as a full general.

own ability to function. By extension, if the Earl of Stair and his staff had remained within the royal vicinity, they also would have had to forgo the use of their horses. Given this, it should be assumed that despite his horse having bolted at the beginning of the battle, the almost sexagenarian monarch was then found an alternate, and no doubt more placid, mount.

A second anecdote regarding the royal personage during the battle is that he took command of the army: he was a king, and thus outranked Stair, who was but an earl. After the battle, opponents of the government policy to Hanover would lament that King George had chosen to wear the uniform of a Hanoverian general officer and not a British one. Attempts have been made to defuse this assertion by saying that he wore a British uniform, but with a Hanoverian sash and insignia. King George himself would later state that he was proud to have worn the same uniform coat that he had last worn at the Battle of Oudenarde in 1708. If we accept that the king was correct in his recollection, then he would indeed have been wearing a Hanoverian uniform coat, as the battle in question was fought several years before the constitutional crisis that saw the accession of his father to the British throne, and his own elevation as Prince of Wales.

With the Allies having begun their advance, there was little that the Duc de Gramont could now do apart from wait. His troops were in their allotted positions, and shortly, his 16 guns would begin to engage the enemy ranks. Naturally, all depended upon de la Vallière and the heavy artillery concealed on the heights around Mainflingen. If they could cause great execution amongst the enemy ranks, the shock of first contact when he launched his own attack would be that much greater and more effective. If he felt any misapprehension at his now being on the wrong side of the Forchbach, then it is not recorded; after all, he had the cream of the French army under his command. He would show his uncle that attack was indeed the best form of defence, and reap the rewards accordingly.

If anything, it was the Allied commanders themselves who at this stage would have been more justified in indulging in bouts of overconfidence as to how the battle would end. At their final council of war, it had seemed that they would have to fight their way across the defiles in the teeth of a hail of defensive fire from an entrenched opponent. Instead, the enemy obliged them by giving up the better ground, coming to meet them head-on.

For the Allied infantry, it was not just the progress through the wheat fields that they found tortuous, but the summer heat itself, making the weight of the thick woollen coats they wore that much harder to endure. But each pace forward brought them one pace closer to the enemy, one pace closer to their being able to vent their anger and frustration as much as their relief at the arrogance that had brought their enemy to forsake their defences and meet them bayonet to bayonet. Steadily, but with unsure footing, they continued their advance, the leading ranks breasting the chest-high crops, and the succeeding ranks continuing to trample the unripe harvest, creating an uneven carpet that would partially mitigate the effects of the furrows beneath their feet. Stopping regularly for officers and NCOs to dress their ranks and allow stragglers to catch up with their parent units, progress was difficult. Soon, however, instead of an anonymous mass to their front, officers would be able to make out the presence of individual units, their brightly coloured ensigns and standards rising above their silent ranks.

Dettingen, by Henri-Louis Dupray. Here, the British infantry close with the enemy before unleashing a deadly volley.

At Noailles' headquarters, the news of Gramont's blatant disregard for his orders was met first with incredulity, then with anger at the abandonment of the Forchbach position. But despite this, the marshal balked at sending fresh orders to his errant nephew, instructing him to comply with original instructions. This was, however, not an act of indecision, but rather one of military pragmatism based upon how armies of the period manoeuvred and operated. It had already taken Gramont some hours to get his troops into their new positions, and would therefore inevitably take as much, if not more, time to reverse this movement. If an officer were to be immediately sent to his headquarters, such a courier would still need to first reach Seligenstadt and then cross the Main – presumably by one of the pontoon bridges – before passing Dettingen and seeking the duke's own position before he could deliver the countermanding orders. This could easily take the better part of an hour. Then, assuming that there was no dissent from the recipient, further orders would need to be drafted and issued, and the troops of the blocking force set in motion.

The problem was that the Allies were by now far closer to Dettingen than they had been at daybreak, and it was almost a certainty that they would have been able to close with the Frenchmen before they themselves could have reoccupied their original positions. Noailles had no other option than to trust in both the ability and fighting spirit of the troops under Gramont's command to defeat the enemy on ground that was most definitely not of his choosing. The only positive that could still be taken from this most dangerously fluid of situations was that his trump card was still yet to be played: de la Vallière – the veteran artilleryman – was still concealed in the heights near Mainflingen, waiting for when he, and he alone, decided it was the optimum moment to pour fire into the enemy's exposed flank. Resigned to his nephew's flouting of his orders, Noailles became now more dependent upon the anticipated effect of his heavy cannon as they bombarded the enemy brigades, raking them with an enfilade fire to which they could not respond.

To put it simply, in order to reach their objective at Hanau, the Pragmatic Army had to keep moving forward. If it stopped, or its advance were to stall or encounter any form of delay, then de la Vallière's guns would punish them. The important thing was that Gramont held them in position long enough to let the French artillery complete its task. Without the benefit of the defensive terrain, Gramont's losses would undoubtedly be higher than were desired or had been originally anticipated – but if a higher 'blood price' would need to be paid to achieve victory, then so be it.

## THE JAWS CLOSE

From his position near Mainflingen, the 74-year-old Jean-Florent de la Vallière, France's most senior artilleryman, alternated between consulting his pocket watch – it was by now approaching midday – and studying the enemy ranks through his telescope. Judging the moment to be right, he signalled to a nearby aide, who walked over to a waiting gun captain. Within moments, the signal gun boomed out, the sign for the concealed batteries to be uncovered and readied for action. Whether the crack of the single discharge was heard or remarked upon by the troops on the far side of the Main is a moot point, but as the sound faded, it was eclipsed by the firing of 40 heavy cannon, their 12lb shot arcing over the river and slicing into the flank of the marching Allied troops. As soon as their recoil had ended, the gun crews dragged their pieces back into position and began the process of loading once more.

The Main River, looking west towards Mainflingen, site of de la Vallière's concealed 12lb batteries.

For de la Vallière, the wisdom of Noailles' decision to place his heavy batteries on the river bluffs was more than justified, as there was no need to aim the cannon, and the crews needed simply to maintain their rate of fire. On higher ground, and with the guns themselves being fired at a slight elevation, the French round shot would reach its apogee somewhere over the water-meadows on the far bank. The effects of gravity meant that some shot would inevitably slice into the enemy formations, whilst others would descend upon them from above. With their considerable range, it also meant that de la Vallière's batteries would be able to play upon almost the entire battlefield, and thus – by definition – the whole of the Pragmatic Army would be dominated by his guns.

For almost half an hour, the French cannon played unchallenged upon the enemy ranks, causing numerous casualties at no risk to themselves. As the bombardment continued, however, one of the Allied commanders took the decision to call up a number of guns to engage the enemy artillery in counter-battery fire. This would provide some moral support and relieve the pressure upon the Allied left wing, which was naturally edging away from the danger and threatening to shuffle into the nearest elements of the centre. This manoeuvre is often ascribed as being due to the intervention of King George, but the truth of the matter is that, even at this relatively early stage in the battle, His Majesty had already taken station on the right wing; for him to have issued such orders would have taken longer to implement than was actually the case, and moreover, if he were to try to micromanage the battle, it could only have ended in disaster. We must therefore look for another suitable candidate as the instigator of the possible movement, and the most likely of these would have been the Duke of Cumberland, who was, after all, in command of the affected sector of the battlefield. But irrespective of who actually gave the supposed orders, the whole question of the deployment is an interesting one, especially as the Allied left wing was stacked up in its order of march, and there was little room for the artillery to be brought forward and deployed safely.

A number of contemporary reports do indeed state that 'a battery of artillery' was deployed around Klein-Ostheim in order to engage the French guns in counter-battery fire. As we know where the Austrian and Hanoverian batteries were deployed, we must naturally assume that these were British cannon. This, however, is where the assertion itself founders, for in his *History of the Royal Regiment of Artillery* (Vol. 1, pp. 124–25), Captain Francis Duncan RA categorically states that the field train sent to Flanders in July 1742 consisted of three artillery companies, each of ten 3lb guns, and that of these, a total of 24 were present for service on 27 June 1743. As Duncan worked from the unit's own records, we must assume that he is correct; if so, it is very doubtful that light cannon firing from Klein-Ostheim would have been able to hit targets around Mainflingen. In short, the events described may have happened later in the battle, when the way ahead was clearer, but their actual timing may have been obscured in the confused race to send the first reports to London.

Both on the road, and across the wheat fields, the Allied troops continued their gradual advance. The troops in the fields halted regularly and dressed their ranks, which in turn imposed delays on the leading elements of the left wing. The latter were forced to endure the enemy artillery fire, and rein in their mounts in order to maintain a uniform speed of advance, without

A horseshoe recovered from the battlefield.

which they would have forgone any flank support. Given that the Main had burst its banks but a few months before, it should be assumed that the water-meadows leading down to the river would have been heavy and treacherous going for the Allied cavalry, which in turn would have meant that, in order to avoid this, they would not have deployed in as open a formation as would generally have been the case.

Just as it seemed that the French enfilade fire would prove to be as decisive as it had been devastating, the Duc de Gramont now made a decision that would not only serve to fatally compromise Noailles' original tactical plan, but would just as equally condemn his earlier misjudgement in crossing the Forchbach.

Despite the fact that he could see with the utmost clarity that the enemy was advancing steadily upon his position, rather than retreating in disorder towards Aschaffenburg, and despite the great execution that de la Vallière's batteries were dealing amongst the enemy ranks, Gramont made what was perhaps the greatest of his several errors of judgement. In the face of a numerically superior enemy, he now gave Harcourt the order to forgo all advantages of position and terrain, and instead to advance and attack the enemy. As the infantry of the centre formed their ranks prior to their own advance, the glittering chevaliers of the Maison du Roi prepared to move out along the Hanau road.

Putting himself at the head of two companies of the Mousquetaires du Roi, Harcourt drew his sword and gave orders for the cavalrymen to advance at the walk, gradually increasing their pace from a slow trot to a fast trot, and then to a canter, closing the distance with the British cavalry directly to their front. Watching with anticipation as the Frenchmen moved forward, the Duke of Cumberland now gave orders for his own horsemen to begin their advance, intent on giving the enemy more than a bloody nose. Gradually, the two opposing lines of red-coated cavalry closed with each other. As the distance closed, trumpeters on both sides sounded the charge, riders spurring their horses forward to greater efforts, each man determined to claim the honour of striking the first blow. The ranks of horsemen struck each other with a sound like the crash of thunder, the clash of swords and the discharge of pistols being drowned out by the cries of men and horses. Harcourt himself was wounded almost at the moment of first contact, and taken from the mêlée by the troopers of his escort to have his injury treated. As the second line of French cavalry – the Gendarmerie and the Chevau-légers – added their weight to the combat, the British line buckled, allowing some of the enemy to burst through their line, before reforming to meet the challenge of the elite of the elite, His Most Christian Majesty's Gardes du Corps, who slammed into their enemy with vicious force. Again, the British line ruptured, and then reformed as the third line of French cavalry hit, their regimental organizations disintegrating into a series of small-unit

or individual combats. Officers on both sides sought to rally their men and throw them back into the swirling combat.

In his account of the battle, the future field marshal George Townshend, who was serving as a junior officer, wrote that 'our cavalry were repulsed at first by the Maison du Roy, who attacked with great vigour'.

As the British horsemen of the second line were ordered forward to support their comrades, they too were hit by the enemy cavalry at full gallop, the Frenchmen again bursting through the enemy ranks without actually breaking them. The Mousquetaires now found themselves in the unenviable position of facing off against a brigade of Hanoverian infantry to their front, with two brigades of largely intact enemy cavalry to their rear. All question of bravery or élan aside, it was clear to the Frenchmen that whilst they had cut their way this far, it would be tantamount to suicide to mount a frontal attack against formed enemy infantry. Their only reasonable course of action – and as hazardous as it would be – was to retrace their steps, and trust that the continuing mêlée between the British and the remainder of their comrades would give them the opportunity to fight their way to safety.

**ABOVE LEFT**
Reconstruction of the uniform of a trumpeter of the Gendarmerie de la Garde. (Copyright and reproduced with kind permission of Gabriele Mendella)

**ABOVE RIGHT**
Reconstruction of the uniform of a drummer, 2e Compagnie des Mousquetaires du Roi. (Copyright and reproduced with kind permission of Gabriele Mendella)

**FIRST BLOOD (PP. 60–61)**

Having disobeyed his initial orders to remain north of the Forchbach, Gramont sought to negate his numerical inferiority and gain a decisive advantage by crushing the Allied left flank before the remainder of the Pragmatic Army could come into action.

Placing himself at the head of the Mousquetaires du Roi, the Duc d'Harcourt (**1**) led the cream of the French cavalry (**2**) against two seemingly fragile lines of British horse and dragoons (**3**). Although the duke was wounded during the early stages of the combat and taken to the rear for treatment, the Musketeers

crashed through the enemy horsemen. Although the latter buckled under the French assault, crucially they did not break.

As successive waves of French cavalry became embroiled in the fighting, the adverse terrain on either side of the Altestrasse meant that they were unable to use their advantage in numbers. Thus, the mêlée degenerated into a grinding and indecisive combat, which would last for almost the whole duration of the battle, with neither side being able to gain the upper hand. The combat was finally broken off when Gramont issued orders for his troops to disengage and withdraw north of the Forchbach.

The immediate problem was naturally the proximity of the Hanoverian infantry. Whereas an ambitious or adventurous commander might be tempted to advance his troops at the quick step, in order to give the enemy a volley at close range (exactly as the British would do at Fontenoy almost two years later), the enemy infantry remained stationary, thereby posing a tacit rather than an actual threat to the Frenchmen. Sawing on their reins, the men of the Maison Rouge turned their horses, and, far fewer in number than when they had started their advance, made their way back to the French lines.

Although the French cavalry would make several charges later during the battle, these would mainly be local, limited affairs, and this, their first attack, would prove to be their most successful. The penetration deep into the enemy flank offered potential reward in the form of a devastating attack on the now-open flank of the enemy centre. But such success came at a price, and it was one that was paid not only in terms of men and horses, but also in terms of tactical advantage. Even as they began their advance, they began to mask the view of de la Vallière's artillerymen, and one by one the batteries ceased firing, not as Noailles had desired – through the expenditure of ammunition – but rather for fear of hitting their own men. Thus, at a time when the French gunners should have been directing as much fire as possible into the enemy's open flank, the Allied troops were being shielded by their erstwhile attackers.

Von Monroy's Hanoverian brigade would unfairly suffer during the later debate regarding their countrymen's bravery, or lack thereof, speculation that had no bearing on the current situation. The truth of the matter is rather tragic: at some time during the advance, a French 12lb round shot had struck the brigade staff and badly wounded Monroy, who lost a leg and would later die from his wounds. His son, serving as an aide-de-camp, was hit by the same ball and likewise had a leg carried off by the ricochet. Both men were buried after the battle in a local church, which itself was destroyed by Allied bombing during World War II.

View from the Allied centre towards the French positions. The woods in the background were planted after the battle.

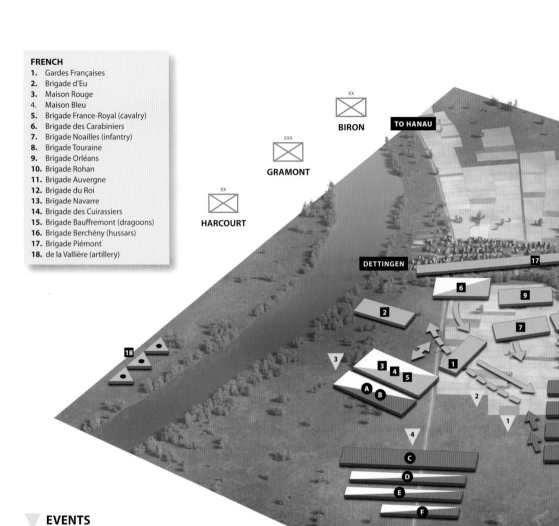

**FRENCH**

1. Gardes Françaises
2. Brigade d'Eu
3. Maison Rouge
4. Maison Bleu
5. Brigade France-Royal (cavalry)
6. Brigade des Carabiniers
7. Brigade Noailles (infantry)
8. Brigade Touraine
9. Brigade Orléans
10. Brigade Rohan
11. Brigade Auvergne
12. Brigade du Roi
13. Brigade Navarre
14. Brigade des Cuirassiers
15. Brigade Bauffremont (dragoons)
16. Brigade Berchény (hussars)
17. Brigade Piémont
18. de la Vallière (artillery)

BIRON

TO HANAU

GRAMONT

HARCOURT

DETTINGEN

ALTESTRASSE

TO ASCHAFFENBURG

▼ **EVENTS**

1. Whilst the Allied centre continues its forward advance, the Gardes Françaises complete their wheeling manoeuvre, which places them upon the Allies' open left flank. As the Frenchmen launch their charge, the left-flank companies of the Allied second line are refused, thus forming a tentative firing line, whilst detachments are withdrawn from the third and fourth lines – under Salm and Clayton – in order to counter-charge the guardsmen and break up the enemy attack.

2. The French attack stalls as the Gardes find themselves fired upon from their front and, more tellingly, from their own open flank, as Salms' troops deliver a pair of short-range volleys and then, as the enemy begins to recoil, launch their own bayonet attack. The French attack collapses, and despite popular myth, the brigade does not disintegrate in flight towards the Main. The effect of the Allied counter-attack is such that the Gardes Françaises are rendered hors de combat, and take no further part in the battle, immediately reducing the number of Gramont's effectives by almost 12 per cent.

3. Closer to the Main River, the cavalry mêlée remains inconclusive, with neither side able to gain a decisive advantage.

4. The Brigade des Carabiniers is unable to deploy for combat, whilst the remainder of the Allied left remains stationary, as Monroy's brigade continues to re-establish its command structure.

5. On the eastern part of the battlefield, Stair's infantry brigades are marching parallel to Arenberg's division, and are preparing their own attack on the French positions. The British foot in the front line are supported by a brigade of Hanoverian foot, with Wendt's Hanoverian dragoon brigade thrown out on the extreme end of the line, both to cover the Allied baggage train and to dissuade the enemy dragoons and hussars from undertaking any aggressive action.

6. Having seen the ignominious failure of the Gardes' attack, Gramont now resolves to engage and rout the enemy centre before either of the Allied flank columns can play a decisive role in the battle. Ordering the infantry line forwards, he also calls upon Harcourt to replicate the earlier infantry attack, and wheel the Carabiniers into the enemy's open flank – seeking to break them, whilst the infantry hold them fixed in position.

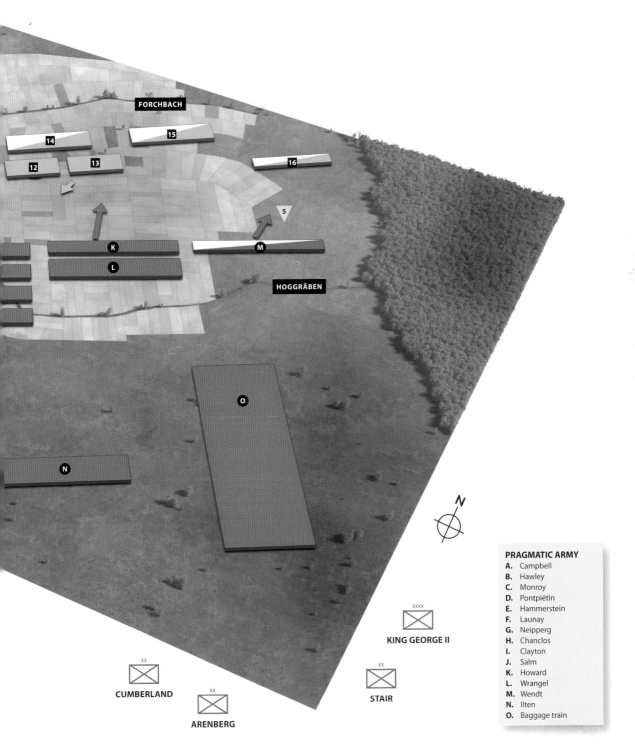

Note: the area shown is 2.28 × 1.6km

FORCHBACH

14   15

12   13   16

5

K

L

M

HOGGRÄBEN

O

N

N

XXXX
KING GEORGE II

XX
CUMBERLAND

XX
ARENBERG

XX
STAIR

**PRAGMATIC ARMY**
**A.** Campbell
**B.** Hawley
**C.** Monroy
**D.** Pontpiétin
**E.** Hammerstein
**F.** Launay
**G.** Neipperg
**H.** Chanclos
**I.** Clayton
**J.** Salm
**K.** Howard
**L.** Wrangel
**M.** Wendt
**N.** Ilten
**O.** Baggage train

A contemporary German print showing the flight of the French army across the Main River in the wake of their defeat.

# THE DUCKS OF THE MAIN

As the cavalry combat developed and grew in intensity, the men of the Gardes Françaises now began their own advance. Having moved a short distance forwards, they then pivoted on their left axis, wheeling round and using the momentum of the movement so as to threaten the open left flank of the Allied centre, whose infantry brigades would be pinned in position and, being unable to manoeuvre effectively, would find themselves engaged from front and flank. An indirect and beneficial effect of the Gardes' advance was that a gap was created in the French line, through which their cavalry could withdraw and reform in relative safety before launching further attacks.

Engaged to their front by three enemy brigades – Auvergne, Touraine and Noailles – and with the advent of this new danger to their left, the troops of Arenberg's sector were in a precarious situation. In normal circumstances, the threat to the flank would be dealt with by the redeployment of supporting elements, but in this case the closeness of the three lines of Allied troops to each other, and the fact that the brigades were deployed in a line of single battalions, meant that their room to manoeuvre was severely restricted. The only option available would be to order the leading brigades to refuse their left by redeploying their end battalions to face the advancing Frenchmen – presumably one battalion from each of the second and third lines (Wolfenbüttel and Duroure respectively) and (given the greater space to redeploy) either one or two battalions from the fourth line (Arenberg, Salm and/or Heister). This ad hoc solution would naturally generate its own problems. Instead of a homogenous command, it would be a line of troops drawn from different parent formations, a state of affairs that could lead to myriad problems with regard to questions of seniority. It would also mean that, despite the inferences of Lord Charles Hay at Fontenoy, the French guardsmen would most likely have been faced by a single battalion of British redcoats and either two or three battalions of Austrians, presumably under the command of Graf von Salm.

Reconstruction of the uniform of a lieutenant de Grenadiers des Gardes Françaises. (Copyright and reproduced with kind permission of Gabriele Mendella)

With both sides having reorganized themselves, the Gardes Françaises continued their advance, and upon reaching musket range, dressed ranks and launched their attack. The Anglo-Austrian battalions held their fire until the charging enemy was close, and then delivered a series of volleys at point-blank range that halted the French attack and then forced them to recoil backwards in disarray before the final volley was followed up with a bayonet charge. Interestingly enough, the decision for the Frenchmen to attack with cold steel has been attributed to Noailles' initial orders that the French infantry should only engage the enemy at bayonet point, albeit in a totally different tactical environment. A second excuse that would later gain currency as an explanation for the Gardes' failure to press home from such an advantageous position was that many of the guardsmen were new recruits, with little or no training.

Tradition has it that the entire brigade now turned on its heels and ran for the dubious safety of the Main River, where many of the troops are said to have drowned – either through exhaustion, wounds or a lack of swimming ability. However, if that were the case, a hole would have been torn in the French line of battle that would have been virtually impossible to plug. Perhaps this is an indication that there was a difference in training and experience between the various battalions of the Gardes Françaises: the more experienced battalions recoiled and disengaged, but did reform to some degree, while those newly raised units broke and ran directly away from the threat, towards the Main. In any event, news of the rout quickly gained currency, and even in Paris the guardsmen would have to suffer the sobriquet *Les Canards du Mein* (the Ducks of the Main). The need to expiate the inferred disgrace would lead to their conduct at Fontenoy some two years later.

## LES CANARDS DU MAIN (PP. 68–69)

As the Gardes Françaises began their seemingly irresistible advance into the open left flank of the Allied centre, the troops closest to the point of impact could do little other than to refuse their leftmost elements in order to prevent their being flanked by the enemy.

In an attempt to disrupt the French attack, troops from the Allied fourth line were detached from their parent formations and thrown against the Gardes as they swung round to complete their attack. Closing with the enemy, the Austrian infantry (**1**) delivered a series of close-range volleys before closing with the bayonet.

The result was electric, as the outermost French battalions simply crumbled under the assault. Large numbers of men were swept away towards the Main River, where many of them drowned, overcome by heat, exhaustion or wounds. Tradition has it that the whole brigade was caught up in the rout, being later derided as 'the ducks of the Main' – *Les Canards du Main*. However, the simple fact is that, had Gramont lost the services of almost one-sixth of his army at a single stroke, the battle would have ended there and then, as he had no reserves with which to plug the gap.

# A GENERAL COMBAT

The first hour or two of fighting had been intense, and whilst the Allies were no doubt glad to have breasted the wave of potential disaster that had threatened their left flank, it was also clear to the French commanders – on both sides of the Main – that Gramont's impetuosity had effectively turned Noailles' plan on its head. The French cavalry under the Duc d'Harcourt had severely mauled their Allied counterparts, but they themselves had been bloodied, and needed to reorganize in order to regain their battlefield effectiveness. Without the support of the Austro-Hanoverian horse still trapped behind Monroy's infantry, and despite their resilience in weathering the enemy storm, the British cavalry under Campbell and Hawley were simply too few to take the offensive, and had to restrict themselves to limited counter-attacks designed to wear the enemy down.

As has been seen, the French guards had been repulsed, but the question that remains to be answered is the extent of this reverse. If the brigade had indeed collapsed in its entirety, its absence would have meant there was no friendly formation large enough for the French cavalry to have reorganized and reformed behind. This supports an assertion that the core of the brigade held firm, otherwise there were but two routes by which the fleeing infantrymen could have reached the dubious safety of the Main River. The first of these would have taken them directly in front of the French cavalry, at a time when they were preparing to launch a second attack on the enemy, and then through the Brigade d'Eu, which was now anchoring the French right flank. Alternatively, it would have taken them directly into the path of the British cavalry, which would more than likely have been unable to resist such

A British print commemorating Thomas Brown's feat of bravery at Dettingen.

a tempting target. The most logical conclusion would therefore be that the Gardes Françaises did actually fracture, and that the rump of the brigade remained on the battlefield.

Around Mainflingen, de la Vallière's initial contribution to the battle had been effective but because of Harcourt's charge, ultimately indecisive – the most important effect having been the temporary paralysis of Monroy's brigade following the death of its commander. But now, and despite the care that had been taken in the placement of his batteries, he had no current targets. A number of cannon on the extreme right of the gun line had already been redeployed so as to be able to engage the rearward part of the enemy left flank, but these were no more than a nuisance. The real task lay with the remainder of his guns. Despite the situation, the latter could not be redeployed, firstly due to the time that would be necessary to complete such a manoeuvre, but also because a sudden development either way could easily uncover fresh targets, which would need to be immediately engaged in order to support a French advantage or disrupt an Allied one.

Trooper Thomas Brown of Bland's Dragoons being knighted by King George II. The artist is S. P. Beadle.

If any of the combatants had forgotten the importance of the twin causeways across the Forchbach, these initial hours of fighting had soon reminded them of what was at stake. For the Allies, it had always been a case of victory resting upon their ability to force a passage across the stream; anything else would result in defeat, and perhaps the loss of the army and its royal commander. But now, and contrary to all initial plans and anticipations, the French were in an almost identical situation: if they failed to maintain possession of both crossings, then they too faced the spectre of an abject surrender. For both sides, all questions of grand strategy and tactics were evaporating like an early morning mist, and the only way to resolve the matter was a slugging competition, with the victor being the last man standing, the army in possession of the field when the last shots were fired. With an almost tangible intake of breath, the two armies now began to close with each other, along the whole length of the battle line.

With his wound now dressed, Harcourt again launched the French right flank cavalry in an attempt to break the enemy squadrons to their front. But instead of the original two lines, they now encountered a single mass of British cavalry. As the two formations collided, and despite their numerical superiority, the French horsemen were unable to repeat their earlier success and break through the British lines. Instead, a swirling mêlée developed, and it was here that trooper Thomas Brown of Bland's Dragoons saw his regimental colours falling to the ground after their bearer had been killed by an enemy cavalryman. Galloping through the press, Brown dismounted in order to retrieve the fallen standard, but as he did so, a Frenchman riding past slashed at him, cutting off two fingers from his left hand. By this stage an enterprising member of the Gendarmerie had sought to make a name for himself by seizing the flag; but after engaging the man in single combat, Brown emerged victorious. His own horse having bolted in the meantime, the Englishman now grabbed a loose mount, and despite his wound, was able to lift himself into the saddle, wedging the flagstaff underneath the saddle girth and holding it in place with his leg.

Determined to carry his prize to safety, Brown galloped through the confused fighting, receiving eight sabre cuts to his face, head and neck – one of which sliced from his forehead through his eyebrow, whilst another carried off most of his nose. Undeterred, he wove his way through his opponents, and eventually reached the safety of the bulk of his regiment, where it was found that (unknown to Brown) he had also been hit by two pistol balls to the body, with a further three shots having passed through his hat. Tradition has it that for his bravery in saving the regimental colours, Brown would be created a knight banneret after the battle, although *Cockayne's Peerage* (1911, pp. 572–73) lists the following as recipients of this honour at Dettingen: the dukes of Cumberland and Marlborough; the Earls of Stair; Dunmore, Crawford, Rothes and Albemarle; generals Honywood, Hawley, Cope, Ligonier, Campbell, Bland, Onslow and Pulteney; and finally Colonel John Huske. Apart from the latter, the list comprises all British general officers who survived the battle – with Huske being promoted to major-general in July 1743. This is not to say that Brown was not honoured by the king: the fact that he would be able to retire from the army shortly after the Dettingen campaign, and was financially able to set himself up as a publican, would tend to support some form of reward. Given the rank inherent in the title of banneret, it may be that he was perhaps given an ordinary knighthood, and that over time, the accounts of the two creations became blurred.

Whereas the initial French cavalry charge had singularly failed to break their British opponents on the Allied left, it seemed as if their second such endeavour would now succeed. After the first round of combat, the Frenchmen had been able to withdraw and disengage, pulling back through the gap caused by the advance of the Gardes Françaises in order to reform,

Although this plan of the battle was printed in Frankfurt, the multilingual text and a number of geographical errors would suggest a British or French cartographer.

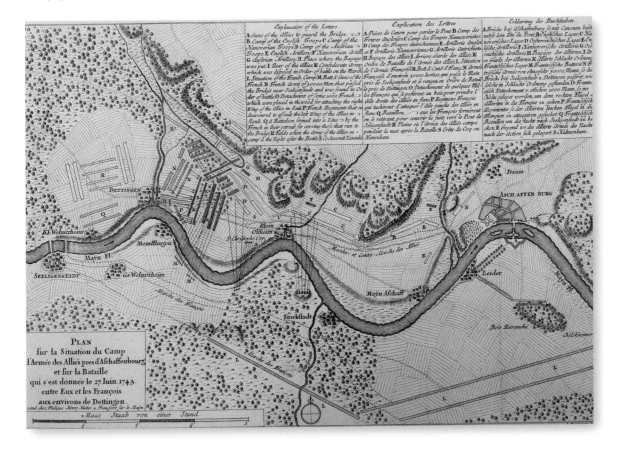

View from the French right towards the Allied centre. Local records indicate that the Spessart Hills (in the background) were not as heavily forested then as they are today.

but Cumberland's cavalry had had no such opportunity to reform. Behind them, Monroy's immobile Hanoverians blocked any possible movement rearwards, whilst the wheat fields behind the Allied centre offered no real option for them to reorganize their ranks unmolested by enemy action.

Once again, the two bodies of horsemen clashed, and once again the British lines fragmented and buckled, but refused to break. In the maelstrom of combat, Ligonier's horse were almost overwhelmed by the French charge, with the commanding officer, Lieutenant-Colonel Francis Ligonier, the general's younger brother, being wounded as he rode at the head of the regiment, whilst Cornet Henry Richardson – carrying the colonel's colour – was seemingly targeted by a knot of enemy horsemen seeking to bring back a trophy for their unit. In a bout of fierce hand-to-hand fighting, Richardson's escorts were killed, whilst he was himself wounded a reputed 37 times by blade and bullet. Elsewhere in the swirling mêlée, Trooper George Daraugh of Rich's dragoons would perform a similar service for his regiment, recapturing its colours after they had been taken by the enemy.

Wounded a second time, Harcourt again gave orders for the cavalry to withdraw and reform before throwing them back into combat, whilst – again – the British were obliged to resolve their situation as best they could. After the battle, the numbers of casualties would suggest a more uneven nature to the intense cavalry combat, but that would be after the level of casualties had been computed and stragglers had returned to the ranks. Having charged the enemy twice, and in greatly superior numbers, the French were seemingly in the ascendant, with Harcourt believing – and possibly rightly so – that all he had to do was to continue to mount the pressure on the enemy horse. If the Maison and her supporting brigades could continue fighting as they had done so far, it was inevitable that the Allied cavalry formation would rupture one final time, and be unable to reform. It would be the landing of one last hammer blow that would smash the enemy flank; and with the Brigade d'Eu and the rump of the Gardes Françaises supported by the remainder of the France-Royal cavalry facing off against Monroy's Hanoverians and their supporting cavalry brigades, the rest of his command would be able to wheel eastwards and then take the Allied centre in both flank and rear. It was an ambitious thought, but one – given the current situation – that was not too implausible. All that Harcourt needed to do was to sweep the battered enemy horsemen aside.

## A WINDOW OF OPPORTUNITY

Buoyed by reports from his right flank, and despite the reverse suffered by the Gardes, Gramont would seem to have believed that one hard push would throw the enemy back on their heels and win the day for France. All he had to do was to order the charge and sweep the enemy aside at the point of the bayonet, exactly as he had been ordered to do a (seemingly long) few hours before. In terms of numbers, Gramont believed that he had sufficient men to hold the enemy right, whilst he himself would lead the remainder of his command against the Allied centre. All told, he had seven brigades of infantry at his disposal, supported by the brigade of cuirassiers and a brigade of dragoons. The hussars under Berchény could make a nuisance of themselves by demonstrating against the enemy's open flank and causing the Allies to divert troops to counter the possible threat.

On the left, the duke's brother-in-law, the Duc de Biron, would take the infantry brigades Auvergne, Roi and Navarre forward, together with the two cavalry brigades, and contain the enemy right; whilst the duke himself took the remaining four brigades (Touraine, Noailles, Rohan and Orléans) against the Austrians, fighting an infantry battle in the centre of the field. With the promised support from Harcourt, he would break his opponents before Tingry – coming up from Aschaffenburg – had time to intervene.

The inherent problem with Gramont's new battle plan was that – once again – he would be giving orders for his troops to mask the French artillery – this time, those batteries deployed in his direct support. As Harcourt's cavalry could do nothing other than wheel directly in front of one of the two batteries in question, we must assume that they were ordered to limber up in the hope of their being brought forward to support the successful attack, once sufficient space had been cleared to their front.

As the French drums sounded the advance, the officers hustling their men forward, the white-coated Austrians to their front now halted. Upon the instructions of their officers, they held their muskets at the ready, two evolutions away from opening fire. As they did so, their gunners brought their pieces forward as fast as they could through the unharvested fields, unlimbering them and clearing for action. The minutes ticking by, it was a nerve-wracking time for the ordinary soldiers on both sides, unable to see the enemy and therefore gauge how close or how far away they were. They would be firing blindly ahead, dependent upon their mounted officers, who – at a higher elevation – naturally had a better view of the battlefield.

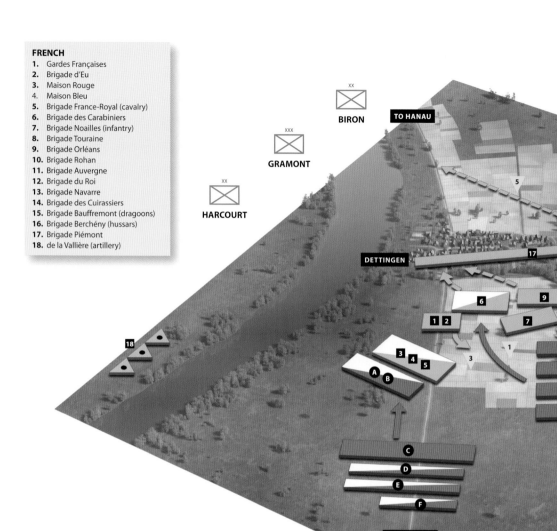

## FRENCH

1. Gardes Françaises
2. Brigade d'Eu
3. Maison Rouge
4. Maison Bleu
5. Brigade France-Royal (cavalry)
6. Brigade des Carabiniers
7. Brigade Noailles (infantry)
8. Brigade Touraine
9. Brigade Orléans
10. Brigade Rohan
11. Brigade Auvergne
12. Brigade du Roi
13. Brigade Navarre
14. Brigade des Cuirassiers
15. Brigade Bauffremont (dragoons)
16. Brigade Berchény (hussars)
17. Brigade Piémont
18. de la Vallière (artillery)

BIRON

GRAMONT

HARCOURT

TO HANAU

DETTINGEN

ALTESTRASSE

TO ASCHAFFENBURG

## ▼ EVENTS

1. As the French line advances to contact with the Allied centre, and a general combat ensues, the Duc d'Harcourt advises Gramont that he is unable to fulfil his orders, as the inconclusive cavalry mêlée to his front means that the Carabiniers lack the requisite space from which to deploy and then launch a flank attack on the Allied centre.

2. Outnumbered, and without the necessary mounted support for his planned attack, Gramont is more than aware of the danger in which he has placed his command. He thus decides to attempt a disengagement and withdrawal across the Forchbach, before the enemy can commit his full strength. Couriers are sent to both Biron and Harcourt, informing them that they are to hold their positions whilst the army centre filters behind them and crosses the stream. At that point, they are themselves to conduct an orderly retreat, with the whole command reassuming a defensive position, as per Noailles' original orders.

3. With the flight of the Gardes Françaises, the Brigade d'Eu has withdrawn slightly, so as to best cover the western causeway and facilitate Gramont's instructions. On the opposite side of the battlefield, French success (Auvergne has overrun an Austrian battery, and is manhandling a captured cannon to the French start lines) has meant that they are dangerously close to the Allied right flank, and the likelihood of Biron's command being able to withdraw without hindrance is increasingly unlikely.

4. In order to regain the initiative, Biron launches the Brigade des Cuirassiers at the British line to his front. As the French horsemen close to contact, the Royal North British Fusiliers (their principal target) refuse their central firings, thus creating two inverted L-shaped formations. As the cavalrymen ride into the gap, they are raked by close-range musketry from both flanks.

5. Disorganized, the troopers mill about ineffectually in front of the red-coated infantry. After another volley, they retreat towards the eastern causeway, having achieved their objective and gained time for the infantry brigades to pull back across the Forchbach.

6. With both sides fully disengaged, and no sign of Tingry's command moving up towards the Allied rear, Gramont takes stock of the situation. Given the disparity in numbers, and the fact that his best troops have been badly mauled, he gives orders for the troops to retire to the pontoon bridges, and to fall back upon Seligenstadt. This effectively concedes the battle to the Allies, who, with the enemy falling back before them, make a concerted push for each of the two causeways, taking a considerable number of the enemy prisoner.

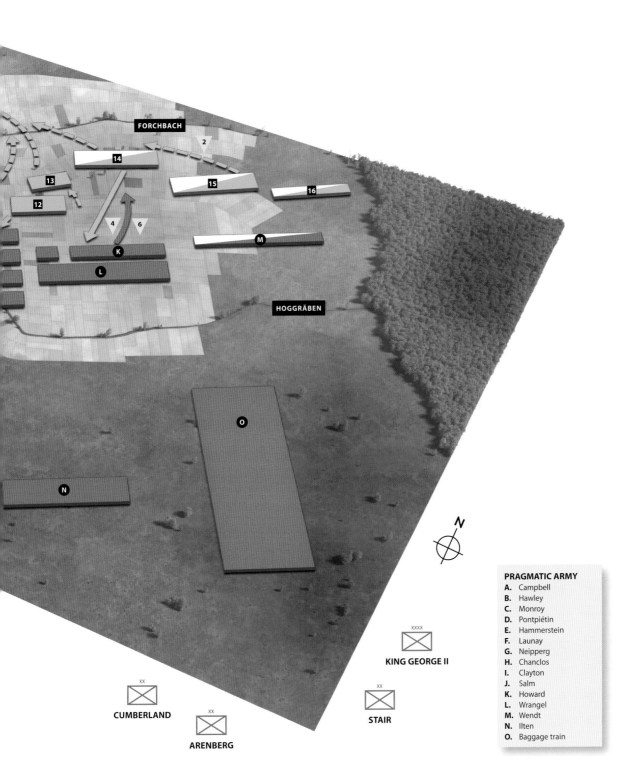

'SAUVE QUI PEUT'
The French attack and collapse, *c.* 12.45pm–2.30pm

Note: the area shown is 2.28 × 1.6km

FORCHBACH

HOGGRÄBEN

KING GEORGE II

CUMBERLAND

ARENBERG

STAIR

**PRAGMATIC ARMY**
**A.** Campbell
**B.** Hawley
**C.** Monroy
**D.** Pontpiétin
**E.** Hammerstein
**F.** Launay
**G.** Neipperg
**H.** Chanclos
**I.** Clayton
**J.** Salm
**K.** Howard
**L.** Wrangel
**M.** Wendt
**N.** Ilten
**O.** Baggage train

View from the sculpture of *die Rotröcke* on the extreme right of the Allied line; the author and Robert Hall provide a sense of scale.

On Gramont's right flank, Harcourt had once again launched his troopers at Cumberland's cavalry, intent on breaking them before moving in support of the central attack; but, as before, the Frenchmen were unable to break their British opponents. The reason for this lay in the fact that the area being fought over had gravitated northwards as the Frenchmen had withdrawn and reformed for their second charge of the day. Consequently, the French had less room in which to deploy, and their largest formation, the Carabiniers, was effectively held in place until more space could be won. Unable to charge through the water-meadows, as much on account of the position of the Brigade d'Eu as of the waterlogged ground underfoot, the French were also obliged to contract their frontage, thus negating their numerical superiority. It was a similar situation that both armies would encounter at Fontenoy two years later, when it came down to passing troops through the defile between the village of Fontenoy and the Bois de Barry. All Harcourt could do was to attempt to wear the enemy down before bludgeoning his way through their ranks, and completing his promised attack on the Allied centre.

View from the French centre towards the Allied right. The sculpture of *die Rotröcke* can be seen just to the left of the building by the treeline.

On the opposite side of the battlefield, having viewed the lines of red-coated troops to his front, the Duc de Biron knew that he would be in for a hard fight. However, the three brigades under his command were all veteran formations that he had previously commanded in Italy, and he knew that whatever the circumstances, they would give a good account of themselves. His main concern was the obvious need to ensure that his flanking brigade was able to maintain contact with their opposite numbers in the central division. Holding his heavy cavalry as a tactical reserve, he ordered his dragoons to extend his line eastwards, primarily to protect his own open flank, but also to give the enemy concern for theirs.

As the two lines of infantry closed to within musket range, the cavalry on the Hanau road continued to hack and slash at each other, firing pistols at close range, their officers seeking to convert even the slightest of advantages into a manoeuvre that would give them an ascendancy over their opponents. But as the casualties on both sides mounted, it was clear that there was no real advantage to be gained. Whilst Harcourt had the numerical superiority that would allow him to rotate units in and out of combat, the enclosed terrain now favoured the smaller numbers of Allied horsemen, and prevented him from committing his whole strength into the fighting. As a result of this, the doggedness and sheer bloody-mindedness of the British horsemen – no doubt inspired by the presence of their youthful commander, the Duke of Cumberland – held the Frenchmen firmly at bay.

Having scrambled across the Hoggräben, the French infantry hurriedly dressed their lines and resumed their march, halting as the initial Austrian volleys created gaps in their ranks. The latter's fire was not particularly galling, but as the range closed, its accuracy improved and casualties began to mount. Eventually, the French halted and gave fire, the discharge creating a pall of smoke that now lay between the two lines of troops, obscuring the men and concealing the effects of the repeated volleys. Had he but known it, Gramont might have ordered an immediate bayonet charge upon the enemy as Feldmarschall von Arenberg was plucked from his horse by the French fire. The Austrian commander was only lightly wounded, but he still required medical treatment, and naturally changes now had to be made in the Allied chain of command.

At the end of the line, the leading battalions of the Brigade Auvergne – part of Biron's command – discovered that they were directly in front of a battery of Austrian light artillery, whose presence had been concealed by the height of the crops. After firing a ragged volley, they launched themselves at the enemy cannon, in an attempt to close and engage the gunners in hand-to-hand combat before they could fire a deadly round of cannister into their tightly packed ranks. It was a close race, but one that the Frenchmen won. Before they were dislodged by an Austrian counter-attack, they manhandled one of the enemy guns out of its position, and a group of men were detailed to drag it back to the far side of the Forchbach.

The fighting was now general along the line, the light crackle of musketry being punctuated by the deeper booming of the Austrian guns, as both sides sought to obtain a decisive advantage. Gramont was becoming even more reliant upon Harcourt making the necessary breakthrough, in order to turn the Allied left. In short, his troops had left Seligenstadt early that morning with the usual provision of powder and shot, and whilst there may have been some ready ammunition available within Dettingen itself, the regimental trains were still on the far side of the Main. If the fighting was

Detail of the cascabel of a French 12lb cannon. A lion or bacchus denoted a 24-pounder, a medusa a 16-pounder, a bird or rooster a 12-pounder, and so on. (PHGCOM via Wikimedia Commons, CC BY-SA 3.0)

to continue at its current pace, his men would soon be reduced to relying on the bayonet. To all intents and purposes, the French troops were limited to what ammunition they carried on them, or what they could forage from casualties. This is not to say that the Allies were in a better position – but their supply trains were physically closer to the battle lines, and, in theory, more easily reachable. If Harcourt were to fail in his task, and with the bulk of his command surrounded on three sides by both the Forchbach and the Hoggräben, Gramont would have no other option than to attempt to disengage and pull back across the stream, a task difficult enough in what could be considered optimum conditions, but whilst in contact with the enemy it would be almost impossible to execute the manoeuvre without incurring prohibitive casualties.

The decision was quickly made when a courier came to say that, unable to deploy his superior numbers, Harcourt was unable to complete the task that he had been given, and that Gramont should consider ordering a withdrawal. If that were the case, he believed that he still had the men – and more importantly the manoeuvre space – to contain the Allied troops facing him, and cover the retreat of any troops using the western causeway. Faced with this dire summary of the situation, Gramont finally realized that he had gambled for high stakes and lost, and that the only realistic option available to him would be to try to mitigate what now had the beginnings of being a military disaster.

Contrary to what is shown in this contemporary German print, Cumberland was unable to have his wound treated until after the fighting had ended.

The troops of the centre were naturally in the most precarious position, and needed to be moved first. As a result, Gramont scribbled a note to both Biron and Harcourt ordering them to cover the causeways whilst Touraine, Rohan, Noailles and Orleáns passed behind them, making their way to safety.

'The whites of their e' en.' This print appears to show the disastrous charge of the French cuirassiers against the British line.

Another painting shows King George, this time mounted, casually observing the immolation of the French Brigade des Cuirassiers upon the bayonets of the British redcoats.

Likewise, the commander of the Piémont brigade was ordered to bring his battalions forward in order to provide covering fire for the retreating troops.

At this stage of the battle, there is no certainty as to the order in which the initial withdrawal took place, but given the presence of the Brigade d'Eu and the mass of cavalry fighting on the French right flank, it would be more than reasonable to assume that a single brigade from the centre crossed at Dettingen, whilst the remainder filed behind Biron's troops on the left.

As the infantry passed behind Harcourt's cavalry, he launched them in another furious charge against the British horsemen. The latter responded with a similar élan, the two sides clashing in a cloud of dust, striking out with swords or firing pistols at ranges so close that the targets could almost be touched. Again – and despite his cuirass – the duke was wounded, receiving prompt treatment, before gamely riding sword in hand back into the mêlée. On the Allied side, the Duke of Cumberland received a bullet wound to the calf, but in his first battle he shrugged it off, intending on having it dressed later. With the advantage ebbing to and fro, the opposing sides resembled a pair of prize fighters, continuing to strike out by instinct whilst waiting for the bell to sound and grant them a brief respite.

On the opposite flank, Biron – a veteran of such situations – knew that he had to exchange space for time in order to allow the central brigades to traverse the Forchbach and reach the relative safety of the northern bank. The bulk of his command consisted of the infantry brigades Auvergne, Roi and Navarre, and his task was made slightly easier in that – as has been seen – Auvergne had slightly overlapped with the French centre. Thus, a refusal of the end battalions would afford some measure of security, with the dragoon brigade performing a similar function on his own left flank. Biron's problem lay in the need to check the advance of the four British battalions immediately to his front (Royal North British Fusiliers, Huske, Handasyde and Charles Howard), and the only weapon left available to him was the one that he had deployed for such an eventuality, the Brigade de Cuirassiers.

**THE WHITES OF THEIR EYES (PP. 82–83)**

Having received Gramont's orders to withdraw, the Duc de Biron, in command of the French right wing, realized that a significant part of his command was too far away from the causeway to be able to disengage cleanly, and that there was every chance that the British could cut their line of retreat.

To avert this possible disaster, he was obliged to commit his mounted reserve: three regiments of line cavalry, spearheaded by the Royal Cuirassiers (**1**). Their task was to turn the left flank of the British infantry advancing directly to their front.

With the enemy closing fast, Lieutenant-Colonel Sir Andrew Agnew – in command of the Royal North British Fusiliers (**2**) – refused the two central firings of his battalion, so that the troops were deployed in two inverted L-shapes. Obligingly, the French cavalrymen rode directly into the gap between the two groups of redcoats, receiving heavy point-blank fire from both flanks before retiring.

As they withdrew, the troopers took further losses from the British fire, but they had halted the British line, ultimately giving some thousands of their comrades the opportunity to withdraw to safety.

A German print showing the plan (above) of the Battle of Dettingen and its latter stages. Note the Allies storming unhindered across the Forchbach 'morass'.

Ordering the heavy cavalry forward, Biron continued to shepherd his charges on their route to safety, fully aware that any outbreak of panic could easily lead to the collapse of the entire wing, and total disaster. As the enemy horsemen closed, Lieutenant-Colonel Sir Andrew Agnew, commanding the Royal North British Fusiliers on the left of the British line, refused his central firing divisions so as to form his regiment into two inverted L-shapes, exhorting his men: 'Dinna fire till ye can see the whites of their e' en … If ye dinna kill them, they'll kill you.'

Obligingly enough, one of the cavalry brigade's three regiments charged directly into the gap, being raked by close-range musketry as they rode through the British formation, and then a second time as they tried to make their way to safety.

After the battle, King George is said to have ridden over to Agnew and chided him by saying, 'Sir Andrew, I see that the enemy cuirassiers rode through your regiment today'; to which the veteran officer is reported to have given the laconic reply, 'Aye, Your Majestie, but not that many rode oot again.'

Biron's gamble had paid off, but it must also be acknowledged that Agnew's prompt action had not only also saved the British contingent from a potential military disaster, but also a political one, if we accept the narrative that King George spent the entire battle on foot.

85

# THE BEGINNINGS OF RETREAT

Whilst Gramont's intention had been to filter one part of his force behind the remainder, and thus reach safety north of the Forchbach, the first effects of this manoeuvre were not to be felt within the ranks of the French army, but rather within those of their opponents. As the French began to tentatively disengage, all along the Allied line of battle commanders could rest their troops somewhat, whilst they themselves took stock of the situation and sent messages up and down the chain of command. Although several officers would later write that this was, to all intents and purposes, the end of the battle, every drama needs its dénouement, where all of the strands and threads are drawn together – and so with the Battle of Dettingen.

After a number of hours of intense fighting, the cavalry combat on the Allied left would appear to have started to peter out. As the enemy to his front began to withdraw, Lieutenant-General Jasper Clayton put himself at the head of a body of troops intending to seize the near end of the causeway and cut off the retreat of any enemy troops that found themselves on the wrong side of the Forchbach. Leading the advance, Clayton was killed by a musket shot to the head, but his manoeuvre would prove to be ultimately successful in sealing off the westernmost of the two causeways, with the shattered Maison du Roi pulling back towards Dettingen in disorder. In the confusion of the retreat, the 24-year-old Duc de Rochechouart – colonel of the Mortemart infantry – was initially grateful that he had successfully manged to bring the majority of his regiment, part of the Brigade d'Eu, to safety. But when he called upon his men to rally upon the regimental colours, he was told that, in the confusion, the colour party had been separated from the rest of the regiment, and that the regimental flag was still on the wrong side of the stream. Calling for volunteers, the young nobleman drew his sword and ran towards the causeway, followed by a number of his men. Fighting their way through the confusion, Rochechouart and his men found the badly wounded ensign – surrounded by the bodies of his escort, and a number of Allied troops who were more than intent on capturing his precious charge. In the sharp mêlée that followed, the Frenchmen were indeed able to save their regimental colours, but at the price of their commander's life, the young duke falling early in the combat.

On the opposite flank, Biron continued to preside over an increasingly smaller area of the battlefield. As the troops of Gramont's personal command continued with their march, he gave orders for the dragoons and then the cuirassiers to begin their withdrawal to the northern bank, intent on gradually reducing his perimeter and then feeding his brigades across one at a time. But with the British having reformed in the wake of the cuirassiers' attack, the pressure was now increasing to his immediate front, and it was becoming a matter of simple survival. He had followed his brother-in-law's orders for as long as he could, allowing as many troops as possible to make their way to safety, but it was a question of either saving his command or sacrificing it.

Having done all that honour had required of him, Biron chose the former, and we must assume that the Brigade du Roi infantry – of which he was colonel-lieutenant – was the last French brigade to quit the field.

Riding to the king, Stair recommended an immediate pursuit to capitalize upon the enemy's disorder. Others, however, pointed out the

reality of the situation: it was still only early afternoon, and with the armies on opposite sides of the Forchbach, the situation was almost identical to that before the battle had begun. The Allies would still need to force a passage of the causeways in the face of an enemy defence, and the troops would need to be rested, the wounded treated and ammunition replenished before they could even contemplate such a course of action. Stair countered by saying that if their troops were disorganized, then the French were even more so, and that a determined thrust now could only pay dividends. Whether or not the Scotsman reminded those present that the enemy heavy artillery was no longer masked by enemy troops is unrecorded, but despite the potential threat the French cannon posed, the decision was made to wait.

For his part, mortified by his nephew's blatant disregard for his orders, Noailles had already been trying to instil some sense of urgency into the Prince de Tingry, in order that he pose a more direct and latent threat to the Allied rear. Now, and still convinced that the ground in front of Dettingen would see the decisive engagement, Noailles rode hard for the bridgehead, marshalling whatever units he could as a final reinforcement for the troops on the far side of the Main – a force which he now intended to command in person.

'The Retreat'. Viewed from behind de la Vallière's artillery positions, this painting clearly shows the French in panicked retreat across the Main, closely followed by the Allies.

## COLLAPSE

Up until the point that he gave the order to withdraw, Gramont had been confident of success. But having watched his troops struggling back to their original start positions, ones that he now realized could and should have been easily held had he only adhered to his original orders, he was struck by a fatal blow of indecision.

Uniform buttons recovered from the battlefield of Dettingen.

Armies are commanded by officers, and amongst his senior subordinates the casualties had been particularly high, as they had either been leading from the front or covering the retreat. Although many who remained bloodied on the field recommended holding their position, the duke's indecision grew. The original plan had always been to fight an infantry battle with the French forces, mounting limited counter-attacks as the enemy debouched from the causeways, but Gramont had turned this on its head. The battle fought had in reality been a cavalry engagement, one whose course had been dictated by the fighting on the Hanau road. Convinced, therefore, that his position was no longer tenable, and asking Biron to once again cover the retreat, he gave another series of orders that would have seemed inexplicable several hours previously. Seemingly without having decided to inform Noailles of his current situation, Gramont compounded his earlier error by ordering that the troops under his command should withdraw to the bridgehead, and from there make for the safety of the far bank. Here, they would in fact meet the troops coming to their relief.

To all intents and purposes, the Battle of Dettingen was now over. The French had withdrawn in relative disorder, the road to Hanau was now open and the Allied lines of supply were secure. Although the Pragmatic Army had outnumbered Gramont's command, such a numerical advantage could only have been applied if the troops in question could be brought to bear. Here – like the Etruscans in Macaulay's *Lays of Ancient Rome* – the Allies would have been forced to attack piecemeal across two narrow causeways, although it must be said that the ancient warriors did not have to contend with enemy cannon raking them in enfilade.

The French advance and subsequent withdrawal meant that the Allies would not have to pay the blood price that Noailles had set for a crossing of the Forchbach. Although it remains in the realm of speculation as to whether (had Noailles' plan been followed to the letter) the Pragmatic Army would have gone down to ignominious defeat rather than glorious victory, how the Allies themselves saw their victory is best summed up by the fact that the composer Georg Friedrich Händel was later commissioned to produce the *Dettingen Te Deum* and *Anthem* in commemoration of the battle. With everything that had been at stake, the outcome of the battle had truly been a 'miracle on the Main'.

A trumpet mouthpiece recovered from the battlefield.

# AFTERMATH

Whilst Dettingen would prove to be a disaster for France politically, militarily it served to cement the reputation of both the French officer corps and the cavalry arm. The French suffered some 900 dead, 1,760 wounded and an estimated 1,500 captured or missing, for a total of approximately 4,160 casualties – a rate of around 16 per cent. For their part, the Allies acknowledged a loss of approximately 2,000 men. There is no exact record of British losses, but if we deduct the Austrian and Hanoverian casualties – 975 and 549 dead and wounded respectively – the implication is that it would have been somewhere in the region of 470 men.

As has been noted, there was no victorious pursuit after the battle. Quite simply, the Allies were far more preoccupied with getting themselves out of the adverse terrain, and establishing an encampment between Dettingen and Hörstein. It was at the latter, rather than on the battlefield itself, that King George famously 'dined in a show of defiance to the enemy'. It was also there that His Royal Majesty granted a number of awards, prominent amongst these the creation of a number of knights banneret – an award that can only be made by the monarch in person, and then only upon the field of battle. Whilst this act of pageantry was being enacted, Stair was hastily writing a note to Noailles requesting that, as the king wished to press on to Hanau, he would consent to arrange for the burial or medical care of the Allied casualties remaining on the battlefield. In an age of gentlemanly conduct, the French general would naturally accede to Stair's request, but could not do so until the day after the battle, which meant that these unfortunates lay without shelter during a night of torrential rain.

In broader terms, there were – to paraphrase the German author Sebastian Küster – as many reported outcomes for the Battle of Dettingen as there were participants. At Versailles, the battle was initially reported as having been a glorious French victory. It must be acknowledged that although Noailles did not achieve the result that he had sought or believed was within his grasp, he had nonetheless prevented the Pragmatic

*A Glorious Victory* – a pamphlet published in London one week after the battle.

## Whitehall, June 23, 1743.

*This Morning Mr.* Parker, *one of His Majesty's Messengers, arrived at the Duke of Newcastle's Office with the following Letter from the Right Honourable the Lord Carteret to his Grace.*

### Published by Authority.

*Dettingen, June* 27/16, 1743.

MY LORD,

HIS Majesty (God be praised) has this Day gained a very considerable Battle. The French passed the Mayn at this Place, with about Twenty-five Thousand Men, and have been forced to repass it with considerable Loss. I write this from the Village near the Field of Battle, which the French were in Possession of; by which Means we have secured our Conjunction with the Hessians, and Hanoverians, in Number above 12,000, which are within two Leagues of us; and to intercept whom, the French made this hazardous Attempt, which has failed them. His Majesty was all the Time in the Heat of the Fire; but is in perfect Health. The Duke received a Shot in his Leg, which pierced the Calf of his Leg; but the Bone is not hurt: He is very well, and in high Spirits. I must refer the Particulars of this great Affair, till To-morrow, or next Day. General Clayton is killed; and we have taken several General Officers Prisoners, and many Officers of the French King's Houshold in their fine Cloaths. The Army lies all Night under Arms. I am in a Cottage with Marshal Neiperg. The Austrians behaved themselves with great Gallantry: The Duke d'Aremberg is wounded with a Musquet-Shot in the Breast. This is a good Beginning of the Campaign, the Emperor's Auxiliaries having received a very considerable Check; and they were the Aggressors.

I am ever, with the greatest Truth, and Respect,

MY LORD,

*Your Grace's*

*most humble,*

*and most obedient Servant,*

Carteret.

P. S. The Hanover Artillery has had a considerable Share in this Victory. The Battle began at Ten in the Morning, and lasted to Four; when the Enemy repassed the Mayn with Precipitation.

Printed by EDWARD OWEN, in *Amen-Corner.*

[ Price Two pence. ]

## The aftermath of the battle

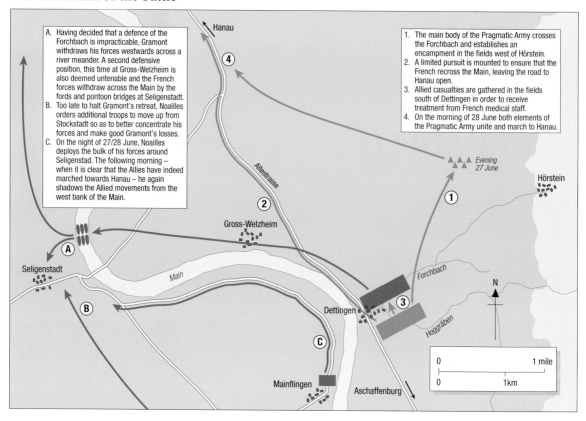

A. Having decided that a defence of the Forchbach is impracticable, Gramont withdraws his forces westwards across a river meander. A second defensive position, this time at Gross-Welzheim is also deemed untenable and the French forces withdraw across the Main by the fords and pontoon bridges at Seligenstadt.

B. Too late to halt Gramont's retreat, Noailles orders additional troops to move up from Stockstadt so as to better concentrate his forces and make good Gramont's losses.

C. On the night of 27/28 June, Noailles deploys the bulk of his forces around Seligenstad. The following morning – when it is clear that the Allies have indeed marched towards Hanau – he again shadows the Allied movements from the west bank of the Main.

1. The main body of the Pragmatic Army crosses the Forchbach and establishes an encampment in the fields west of Hörstein.
2. A limited pursuit is mounted to ensure that the French recross the Main, leaving the road to Hanau open.
3. Allied casualties are gathered in the fields south of Dettingen in order to receive treatment from French medical staff.
4. On the morning of 28 June both elements of the Pragmatic Army unite and march to Hanau.

The gravestone of a French officer killed at Dettingen.

Army from continuing its march into Upper Bavaria, thereby granting a reprieve for the Franco-Bavarian army there. Such indeed was the official government position, and a decree was issued by the French crown forbidding publication of any details of the fighting that contradicted the government's version of events. Such restrictions became almost immediately unenforceable, and society was soon being regaled with lurid accounts of the battle. Later it would be referred to as *la jour des batons rompus* (the day of the broken batons) – a tacit condemnation of the apparent ambition of several senior officers, notably Gramont and Harcourt, whose perceived desire to join the exclusive ranks of the marshalate was deemed to be worth the loss of any number of the troops under their command. In Harcourt's case, the criticism was almost certainly unwarranted.

For Austria, the battle was a sharp lesson in the realities of 18th-century Realpolitik. Decisions that had been made at the highest of levels were effectively tossed aside at a whim, and whilst Vienna could console herself with the conduct of her soldiers on the battlefield, there remained little that she could say or do for fear of upsetting the political apple cart. Some lessons need to be learned the hard way, and for Austria it was that she could only afford to further prosecute the war so long as she could continue to count upon the receipt of foreign subsidies. With France openly supporting Emperor Charles Albert, there remained but one possible source of such military funding. In the hope both of continued financial support, and with the possibility that Great Britain might become a fully fledged ally rather than an auxiliary, such sensibilities had to be carefully observed, and a united diplomatic front maintained, leastways in public.

In Great Britain itself, the battle was reported as being a triumph of British arms over those of its traditional enemy France, with the actions of the other contingents within the Pragmatic Army, even those of the Hanoverians, being relegated to a strictly secondary role. That said, the battle also served as a much-needed public relations exercise for the British monarchy. Rumours were rife as to both the unpopularity of the House of Hanover and a nostalgic sympathy for the exiled House of Stuart, which, despite the religious divide, was at least British in origin. As a result, King George II received his adulation as a warrior-king, the misadventure with his mount being used as a demonstration of his desire to fight amongst the ranks of his soldiers and to share in their dangers. The fact of his being the last British monarch to lead *troops* in the field eventually became transmuted into his being the last British monarch to lead *a British army* in the field – a subtle difference, but one used to great effect domestically.

Several weeks after the battle, the Earl of Stair was asked for his view of the fighting, and answered laconically: 'the enemy made one grave error, whilst we made two.' When asked to elucidate upon his comments, he replied: 'The French were impatient for battle, and that was their mistake. Ours were firstly, to find ourselves in a position where only total victory would save us from total destruction, and then, when granted the victory that we sought, to fail to capitalize upon it.'

Ironic as it may seem, if there were a certain winner of the Battle of Dettingen, it was Emperor Charles Albert himself. It was true that his principal ally had been beaten and his own forces were firmly on the defensive, but in the heady aftermath of victory, he was invited to a private meeting with King George at Worms. There, the British king personally awarded him a significant financial subsidy, much to the chagrin of both London and Vienna, who would ultimately be obliged to reimburse the royal purse.

But the ultimate legacy of the battle was the suffering imposed on the local populace. The manoeuvres of both armies led to an almost total destruction of the anticipated harvest, threatening the local inhabitants with starvation over the winter months, a devastation from which they would not recover for a number of years.

Georg Friedrich Händel, whose *Anthem* and *Dettingen Te Deum* were composed to commemorate the Allied victory. Both pieces were first performed on 27 November 1743 in the Chapel Royal, St James's Palace, London.

The Dettingen battlefield memorial. The inscription admonishes readers: 'Remain at Peace with Each Other'.

# THE BATTLEFIELD TODAY

Throughout the succeeding 275 or so years, much has changed on and around the battlefield of Dettingen. The most immediate aspect is naturally the overlay of a modern transport and communications infrastructure, which on one hand has had a detrimental effect on the battlefield, whilst on the other facilitates a visit to those locations still visible, notably those on the Allied right wing.

The above notwithstanding, the most visible change to the terrain fought over by the two armies is the Main River itself. During the 19th and early 20th centuries, the needs of agriculture and industrialization meant that rivers were often dredged, rechannelled and embanked, so as to ease the passage of waterborne traffic, and to reduce the likelihood of flooding. Today, the river is roughly 90m across from bank to bank, but at the time of Dettingen, it was easily double or even greater in width than that. If we take the Theoderichstor (a water-gate that was used to bring cargo and foodstuffs into the Episcopal Palace at Schloss Johannisburg in Aschaffenburg), the entry port is perhaps 30–40m from the current position of the river, a certain indication of how much the course of the river has been altered over the years. Above the gate there are a number of high-water markers, which show how high the floodwaters were on occasions when the Main burst its banks. Naturally, these markers were emplaced over a number of centuries, but some of them date from the decades before and after the Battle of Dettingen, and reach to the top of the gate itself – a height of about 4.5m. The latter is testament to the scale of inundation that regularly swept across the plain, sustaining the fertility of the soil through water and alluvial deposits; certain ground – if it were needed – for the presence of the numerous drainage channels over which the battle was fought. It should also be noted that these deposits accumulated over the years, and that the ground level at the time of the battle was significantly lower than it is today.

One of the key parts of Noailles' battle plan was the construction of a number of concealed 12lb artillery batteries on the higher ground on the western bank of the Main. From there, they would enfilade the enemy with plunging fire, well within their effective range, whilst the enemy 3lb cannon, at a lower elevation and at the outside limits of their effective range, would be conducting counter-battery fire more for the effect on morale rather than the damage that they could inflict on the French guns. We only know the rough deployment area of the French artillery, but it is again worthwhile to note that as one walks along the pathway to the base of the footbridge to Mainflingen, in 1743 one would already have been up to one's neck in water.

Flanking the Allied march were the Spessart Hills, a line of wooded elevations rising to about 450m above sea level, vying with the Main to be the dominant terrain feature in the area. Although many later sources depict the Spessart as a thickly wooded, mountainous area, modern research would seem to indicate that by 1743, much of the lower levels of trees had been cleared or thinned out by local craftsmen, only being replanted much later. This would naturally suggest that passage across the lower slopes would therefore be less arduous than was previously believed, and would thus substantiate contemporary reports that both the troops of the Allied right wing and the baggage train were able to negotiate this area without an inordinate amount of delay. On a clear day, and from the upper slopes, one can see the whole panorama of the battlefield, from Aschaffenburg in the south to Hanau in the north.

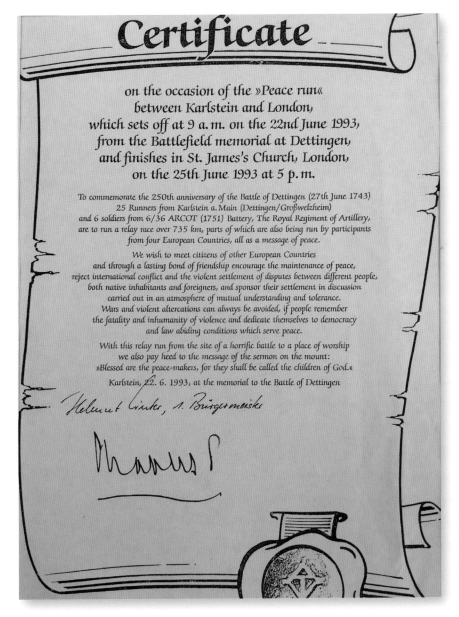

# Certificate

on the occasion of the »Peace run«
between Karlstein and London,
which sets off at 9 a.m. on the 22nd June 1993,
from the Battlefield memorial at Dettingen,
and finishes in St. James's Church, London,
on the 25th June 1993 at 5 p.m.

To commemorate the 250th anniversary of the Battle of Dettingen (27th June 1743)
25 Runners from Karlstein a. Main (Dettingen/Großwelzheim)
and 6 soldiers from 6/36 ARCOT (1751) Battery, The Royal Regiment of Artillery,
are to run a relay race over 735 km, parts of which are also being run by participants
from four European Countries, all as a message of peace.

We wish to meet citizens of other European Countries
and through a lasting bond of friendship encourage the maintenance of peace,
reject international conflict and the violent settlement of disputes between different people,
both native inhabitants and foreigners, and sponsor their settlement in discussion
carried out in an atmosphere of mutual understanding and tolerance.
Wars and violent altercations can always be avoided, if people remember
the fatality and inhumanity of violence and dedicate themselves to democracy
and law abiding conditions which serve peace.

With this relay run from the site of a horrific battle to a place of worship
we also pay heed to the message of the sermon on the mount:
»Blessed are the peace-makers, for they shall be called the children of God.«

Karlstein, 22. 6. 1993, at the memorial to the Battle of Dettingen

Helmut Linker, 1. Bürgermeister

A certificate commemorating the 1993 Peace Run between Dettingen and London. The document is signed by Helmut Winter, former Bürgermeister of Karlstein, and Charles, Prince of Wales.

# BIBLIOGRAPHY

*A Complete List of All His Majesty's Land Forces – Corrected and Made Perfect to the Current Year, 1746*, London, 1746

*A Complete List of the Colonels, Lt-Colonels, Majors, Captains, Lieutenants and Ensigns of His Majesty's Forces on the British Establishment*, London, 1740

*A New Bloody Ballad on the Bloody Battle of Dettingen*, London, 1743

Bland, Humphrey, *A Treatise of Military Discipline* (sixth edition), London, 1746

Bradley, Arthur G., *Wolfe*, London, 1903

Campbell-MacLachlan, Neil Archibald, *William Augustus, Duke of Cumberland*, London, 1876

Charteris, Evan, *William Augustus, Duke of Cumberland: His Early Life and Times (1721–48)*, London, 1913

Coxe, William, *Memoirs of the Administration of the Rt. Hon Henry Pelham* (2 vols), London, 1829

Fortescue, Sir John William, *A History of the British Army* (Part One, vol. 2), London, 1899

Graham, John Murray, *Annals & Correspondence of the Viscount & 1st and 2nd Earls of Stair* (2 vols), Edinburgh, 1875

Hassall, Arthur, *The Balance of Power 1715–1789*, London, 1898

*Historical Memoirs of His Late Royal Highness William Augustus, Duke of Cumberland*, London, 1767

Malbez, Chevalier de, *Campagne de M. le Maréchal de Noialles en Allemagne dans l'Année MDCCXLIII*, Paris, 1892

Mayo, Lawrence Shaw, *Jeffry Amherst: A Biography*, New York, 1916

Noailles Duc de, *Campagne de M. le Maréchal Duc de Noailles en Allemagne l'an MDCCXLIII* (2 vols), Amsterdam, 1760

Pinard, M. (ed.), *Chronique Historique Militaire* (8 vols), Paris, 1760

Porges, August (ed.), *Österreichischer Erbfolge Krieg 1740–48* (vol. 5), Vienna, 1901

Rousset, Camille, *Correspondence de Louis XV et du Maréchal de Noailles* (2 vols), Paris, 1865

Skrine, Francis, *Fontenoy & Britain's Share in the War of the Austrian Succession*, London, 1906

Steiner, Hofrat, Dr., *Beschreibung der Schlacht bei Dettingen am Main (27 Juni 1743)*, Darmstadt, 1834

Stürgkh, Carl Grafen, *Die Pragmatische Sanktion*, Vienna, 1913

Wilson, David A., *The French Army of the War of the Austrian Succession* (vol. 1, second edition), original manuscript loaned by the author

Willson, Beckles, *The Life and Letters of James Wolfe*, London, 1909

Wolf, Adam, *Die Geschichte der pragmatischen Sanktion bis 1740*, Vienna, 1850

# INDEX

Figures in **bold** refer to illustrations.